TOMMO'S YEAR

Tommo's Year

DEREK THOMPSON'S
RACING YEAR

Derek Thompson
with
Colin Cameron

B⬛XTREE

First published 1997 by Boxtree
an imprint of Macmillan Publishers Ltd
25 Eccleston Place, London SW1W 9NF
and Basingstoke
Associated companies throughout the world
ISBN 07522 11218
Copyright © Derek Thompson with Colin Cameron 1997
Photographs copyright © Gerry Cranham, except where listed
below
The right of Derek Thompson and Colin Cameron to be
identified as authors of this work has been asserted by them in
accordance with the Copyright, Designs and Patents Act 1988.
1 3 5 7 9 8 6 4 2
A CIP catalogue record for this book is available
from the British Library
Printed and bound in Great Britain by
Mackays of Chatham plc, Chatham, Kent
Picture Acknowledgements: Plate 1 (top), plate 6 (top), plate 7
(middle), plate 8 (all): Derek Thompson, private collection; plate
6 (bottom): Stare Pictures

To Stanley Moorhouse Thompson
You always said that I should write a book one day.
I wish with all my heart that you were still here to
read it.

Contents

Acknowledgements

I've got to say thank you to the two women in my life: my wife, Julie, and my mother, Lillian. It is not easy dashing from one racetrack to another and life can get pretty fraught at times, but these two keep me on the right track. They put up with a lot and I consider myself very lucky to have these two outstanding human beings on my side.

My brother Howard may not realize it but he is still my best friend, and I would probably still be working on radio if Bob Champion hadn't been – and still is – such a good mate.

A special mention to Andrew Franklin, the producer of Channel 4 Racing, for sticking with me. It is a special feeling, being part of such a winning team. Long may it continue.

Thank you, too, to Sheikh Mohammed and his right-hand man John Leat, who have opened up Dubai. I now consider Dubai my second home and although it entails a lot of travelling it's a pleasure to be part of the Dubai racing scene.

Bob Burrows and Cliff Morgan, both former heads of BBC Radio Sport gave me the original chance to earn my living doing something that I love – reporting on sport, and in particular horseracing.

Liz Hobbs, my agent and the former world water-skiing champion, came up with the idea of *Tommo's Year*. Where she gets her energy from I don't know, but perhaps it's being married to my old pal Frazer Hines.

Colin Cameron somehow managed to put all my ramblings into English. We recorded hours and hours of memories on to his tape machine and we both hope you enjoy the finished product.

Finally, without the help and guidance of my late father, Stanley, I would never have been able to achieve what I have. He was a man I looked up to in every way and a day doesn't go by when I don't think of him. This is for him.

Introduction

I've worked in racing for nearly thirty-five years and in radio and television for about twenty-five. In that time, the sport has provided me with great opportunities, pleasure, thrills, excitement and loads of variety.

Take three weeks in 1996. Saturday, 9 March. Leave Newmarket for jumps racing at Sandown Park. I present *The Morning Line* for Channel 4 and then the afternoon's racing. We focus on the build-up to Cheltenham. Which trainers are in form? Who is riding well? What are the pointers for the Festival?

After Sandown, a flight to Dubai to commentate at Nad Al Sheba racecourse on Sunday's race meeting. Work on the build-up to the Dubai World Cup in a fortnight's time is the priority. The world's best older horses have arrived for the world's richest race. Interviews to be recorded.

Back to Britain for Monday, arriving at 2.30 a.m.

Tuesday, the Cheltenham Festival. Three days of the finest National Hunt racing, three *Morning Lines* and afternoon programmes climaxing with Thursday's Gold Cup. Working at Cheltenham again, just like the old days when I was on Radio 2.

Friday, Fakenham, another 'day at the office' providing commentary for Satellite Information Services betting-shop broadcasts and for subscribers to the Racing Channel. It's a gaffs track to which, thirty years ago, Denys Smith might have sent me with a runner when I worked in his yard. My telephone tipping will hopefully provide callers today with a few winners.

A betting shop to be opened on Saturday, a personal appearance and the chance to meet some new punters. A speech, some jokes.

Flying to Dubai, on Sunday, for five days of filming more interviews and features to go with next week's Dubai World Cup. I present a programme every night, live on the Gulf's English-speaking channel at 9 p.m. Also some time for a jog, a swim in the sea by the Forte Grand Jumeirah Beach Hotel, and maybe some golf. Still mad about all sport after all these years, although I have long since retired from the saddle.

Thursday, the twenty-first, and three days of flat racing at Doncaster, the first meeting of the new season. No *Morning Line*, but three full afternoons of racing. Celebrities and sporting stars are out in force in Town Moor. Frankie, too. Flat racing is back. Brilliant! A chance to meet old friends and make new ones on and off air.

After the Lincoln Handicap in the afternoon, a helicopter, arranged by Sheikh Mohammed's right-hand man John Leat, takes me to Heathrow from Donny so that I can catch a flight to Dubai for the draw for the World Cup on Wednesday. Back at the Jumeirah Beach Hotel once again.

The build-up to the World Cup. Interviews and programmes right up to the race on Wednesday. Social functions every night. Simply Red perform at the Hilton Beach Club, in front of Burt Bacharach and Imran Khan.

Wednesday, the Dubai World Cup and the triumph of the mighty US Champion Cigar. I commentate on the race, an honour.

Back to Britain for the Grand National at Aintree on Saturday. I present the *Morning Line* programme from London before travelling home to Newmarket to enjoy the BBC's excellent coverage hosted by my old Radio 2 workmate, Des Lynam.

Just three hectic weeks from one of my thirty-five years in racing. My racing year has always allowed me to share all the ups and downs, the highs and lows, the sheer variety that, for me, has always featured in every twelve months of the Turf.

JANUARY

Beginnings

Some people wake up on 1 January, New Year's Day, in a sweat thinking about the next twelve months. They are a little apprehensive and nervous of the uncertainty that lies ahead. Especially those with hangovers who might be feeling sorry for themselves. I suppose, in some respects, I'm lucky. Like anyone else, I have the odd moment of self-doubt (and the occasional hangover) but there is less worry for me at the start of the year. At least I already know the racing fixture list. The next twelve months is clearly mapped out – ever since I was a small boy, the racing calendar has played a big part in shaping – and enriching – my life. On New Year's Day I can say, pretty confidently, that I will be at Cheltenham, the home of National Hunt racing, for its first meeting of the new year, with a big Bank Holiday crowd – or, if the weather turns bad, at Windsor for the New Year's Day Hurdle – and the promise of plenty of excitement to come in the months ahead. I hope that will be the case for a long time yet.

When I was young my late father, Stanley, shared his love of horses with me and also taught me all about the racing game. I was born in 1950 in Stockton, County Durham, and I was eight when my father first took me to the local track. It cost four shillings to get in, and although, of course, I was far too young to bet, I loved it. In my early days, we would go racing whenever Dad was free or we would watch it – my brother Howard, too – on television. The day always ended with fish and chips. When I was a bit older I started going on my own to the racecourse, to the Silver Ring, by bus. I'd go whenever I could. Every minute of it was special to me.

Today, I'm privileged to be paid to go racing across Britain, from Ayr to Brighton, from Yarmouth to Bangor, and all over the world, to Dubai for the November to April season, to America, Ireland, France, even Japan and maybe Australia. The boy from Stockton got lucky – at least, I certainly think so.

I owe more than just my interest in racing to my father. He gave me a first start in broadcasting, too. During the Second World War Stanley Thompson was a flight sergeant in the Royal Air Force. He flew with the pathfinders, dropping flares to help the Wellington bombers find their targets. After the war he started up a steel company, which Howard now runs, but his real passion was always racing or, more specifically, hunting and the point-to-point field. Father used to provide point-to-point commentaries and when his eyesight began to fail I helped out more and more until eventually I took over the job.

Howard can vouch for me when I say that I always wanted to be in racing as a commentator and on television. He was there when I said it live on air, I think, at the age of nine. We had gone racing to Redcar and John Rickman, who presented the old ITV 'Seven' – the seven races featured on *World of Sport*, the Saturday afternoon sports programme of the time –

asked some young lads what they wanted to be when they grew up. I honestly said I wanted to work in racing and on television! Bob Champion was with us. He told John that he was going to become a jockey and win the Grand National, which is exactly what he did. Today Bob is one of my best friends. We go all the way back. I first met him when I was six. We grew up together in the north-east and sometimes we hitched a lift to the races on the knacker's wagon, which was driven by Bob's father. I don't remember what Howard said to John Rickman – the video tapes have been, mercifully for me now wiped but, as well as becoming a successful businessman, he went on to become the Master of Foxhounds for the Cleveland Hunt.

Commentating in the sixties was a very different game to what it is now. When I started acting as stand-in for my father at point-to-points aged fifteen, you were not allowed to say certain words and phrases. And these were not even swear words! It is only over time that these restrictive rules were relaxed. But the best commentators of those days were already as good then as they are today. The commentating legends – the Peter O'Sullevans and the Peter Bromleys – have always had a way of saying things. It didn't matter that some words and phrases were denied them: they still had their unique styles and voices.

I still commentate at the racecourse all year round when I'm not covering racing for television. I remember my first racecourse assignment. It was with Cloudesley Marsham, who retired in 1992 but has continued to supply the comments for the in-house television coverage at Ascot. Today racecourse commentaries accompany the Satellite Information Services pictures beamed into betting shops. SIS opened up the commentary world to many new, up-

and-coming broadcasters. The Racing Channel, the cable station that broadcasts its service into the homes of its subscribers, has taken this a stage further – some good new talent has appeared here too. For me, as well as SIS work and Racing Channel duty, an added, and increasingly important, commitment is the commentary at the ruling Maktoum family's Nad Al Sheba racecourse in Dubai, with its six months' racing season throughout the British winter.

As a broadcaster, I graduated through the ranks of radio – local, then nationwide on Radios 2 and 4 – to television with ITV and *World of Sport*, presenting the old ITV Seven. Finally, in 1985, I made the switch to Channel 4: one of the most popular and enjoyable involvements I have today is with *The Morning Line*, the Saturday-morning show that previews the afternoon ahead, looks back at the racing week on Channel 4 and reviews the newspapers – both the national newspapers and those that are local to the racing of the day.

In television broadcasting, I particularly admire Peter O'Sullevan. I wrote to him when he was awarded the OBE and he replied to say that he had accepted the honour on behalf of all commentators and broadcasters. I was delighted when he received a Knighthood in the Queen's birthday honours list of 1997. He has always had so much control at the microphone. I remember how restrained he was in his commentary when Attivo, whom he owned, won the Triumph Hurdle at the Cheltenham Festival in 1974. I don't know how he kept himself in check, knowing that he had just won one of the season's most prestigious and competitive races over jumps at the year's premier meeting. At the start of my career at a point-to-point, my brother was riding in a members' race and half-way up the run to the line I had urged him, 'Go on, Howard,' over the public-address system. I ended up in the stewards' room for a ticking-off.

Graham Goode is at the head of the current generation of commentators, along with the BBC's Jim 'J.A.' McGrath. GG is Channel 4's millionaire. He looks after his pennies and has invested his money shrewdly. He is very laid-back but has a dry sense of humour and is a tough professional underneath a soft exterior. GG's portly English-gent look disguises his hard edge. He is also called the Owl, partly because he has great eyesight but mainly because he looks like an owl! His catchphrase is, 'This is a good horse.' Nothing fazes him – not even silly names: there used to be a horse, trained by Taffy Williams in County Durham, called Mabsabrabcab, but GG was still able to joke with me, then a budding racecourse commentator, about the prospect of calling the horse home. A great professional with a cool head on his shoulders.

I think it was for the best that it was Bob Champion, and not me who decided to become a jockey and try to win the National. I can say with complete confidence that I would never have rivalled him, even if Champ had carried a few extra pounds of weight in his saddle to give me an advantage over him in a tight finish.

My own riding career began in the point-to-point field when I was seventeen and ended, once and for all, about twenty-five years later, in great pain. On my riding début I finished fifth. I had never been so fast. After seven minutes' riding hard I almost collapsed on dismounting. Retirement came to me suddenly on the Newmarket Heath where I normally rode horses in exercise for a few trainers every morning. I fell off a hack on the gallops at Newmarket and broke my wrist. All falls hurt, but some falls really hurt. Julie, my wife, was with me at the time and I'm sure she would vouch for the fact that I was in some pain. In between début and retirement, I rode for David Nicholson and have the blue and silver tie that the 'Duke' gives all his jockeys to prove it. I have also schooled a few on the training ground and even won a race for Nicky Henderson on a horse called Classified. Yes, the same beast who went on to finish third in the Grand National – but not with me in the saddle handicapping his progress – in West Tip's race of 1986. Less distinguished moments include the time when a horse ran away with me at Catterick. It almost took me through the corrugated-iron fence that used to be down at the start for two-mile steeplechases. Once I'd got hold of the brute for the actual race, he buried me at the first fence and left me nearly unconscious.

The fall at Catterick was just one of those things, and I was more concerned about the cost of a new pair of riding boots: the first thing I noticed on regaining my senses was that they had been shredded in the tumble. I have no idea how this happened. After that, I carried on riding, but without any great confidence or improvement in fortunes. The last schooling session – where a horse new to National Hunt racing is taught how to jump fences and hurdles – in which I played a part was shared by Steve Smith-Eccles. He rode the new prospect and I partnered the lead horse, a stable hack. I started off five lengths in front but ended up five lengths behind after one jump. The ten-lengths turnaround suggested to me that it was time to leave the schooling to the professionals, so I did.

The day I enjoyed my finest hour on Classified at Plumpton, I beat HRH, The Prince of Wales. It was 1980. The Prince, who rode one for Ian Balding, was great about it and spoke to the crowd after weighing in along with all the other jockeys. Classified was a certainty to win that day. I had partnered the horse, who was a bit bad-tempered, in a gallop a few days before the race and we had outstripped Steve Smith-Eccles and Nicky Henderson, who were both riding good horses, by about twenty-five lengths, so His Royal Highness was up against it, even though he was on the favourite. All the stable gambled money on the horse – even the head lad, which is serious – so it was lucky I won. I would have been strangled for getting the horse beaten through my riding, but in the race itself, Classified went like the wind. The following day's papers carried another story. I had borrowed a pair of Nicky Henderson's breeches, which for me were pretty figure-hugging. In fact, I couldn't quite get the flies done up before the race and they split open on the run-in. This prompted a newspaper to record the finish of the race under the headline 'The Outsider Who Flashed Past The Prince'. I've still got the photograph.

My efforts to become a trainer were less revealing but ultimately about as successful as my career as a jockey. I was assistant for a while to the now veteran trainer Denys Smith at his Bishop Auckland yard and then for a further six months in France, but, like riding, it was never going to be my thing. At Denys's yard, I was really just a stable lad and I got the tickings-off (sometimes a bit stronger than that!) along with everybody else. They were happy times, though. I got to lead a horse up at Cheltenham. And Brian Fletcher, who rode Red Rum to win the Grand National twice, was the stable jockey who also partnered Red Alligator for Denys to win the race in 1968, five years before Rummy's first victory. The great Irish jockey Paddy Broderick was also riding for the stables then and I used to travel with the pair of them to a meeting when I had a ride in an amateur race.

These times provided great memories for me to enjoy today. My friendship with Denys has withstood the test of time, although there have been moments when it has been strained. I once interviewed Steve Smith-Eccles immediately after a race in which he had ridden one of Denys's. In running the horse had injured himself and, as a result, crossed the finish line quite lame. Denys claimed in a letter to the *Sporting Life* that I made Steve look heartless in the interview. It caused a bit of an argument, but that is all forgotten now. We're still mates. Denys always introduces me to everyone as his 'assistant trainer'. He has about a winner a week on the flat and over the jumps, which is a great achievement for a trainer in the north operating out of a relatively modest-sized yard.

I'd like to think that even my limited experience as a jockey and in a racing yard have been a great help to me in working as a journalist and in broadcasting. I hope that when I am critical of jockeys, they understand that my point is made with some practical understanding of the difficulties riders experience in the course of a race. Similarly, I have seen at first hand how difficult it is to prepare racehorses to run to their very best at the racecourse. It can be tough to accept criticism, but I hope any comments I make about jockeys and trainers are at least considered fair and balanced by them, backed up as they are by my experience of riding and the training yard.

I can certainly claim to have started at the bottom in broadcasting. I began covering the local race meetings for Radio Teesside and would drive the radio car to places like Redcar every Saturday to do an outside broadcast from the track. No one had ever tried this before and I hope these early 'OBs' boosted the sport in the north-east. In 1972, I moved to Radio 2 and was based in the same room – number 3096 – for nearly nine years covering all sports and receiving a real drilling in broadcasting from Angus Mackay, the former producer of Radio 2's *Saturday Sports Report*, now, of course, on Five Live. For Angus, a forty-five second bulletin meant forty-five seconds, not forty-six or forty-four, or even forty-four-and-three-quarters.

The radio sports desk team covered everything, which was a bit frustrating for me as I really wanted only to do racing. We had to read news bulletins and results from the studio, as Five Live carries today, which could be a bit dull. There was a twelve-page document that instructed us on how to read the classified racing results so that it would take twelve seconds per race, allowing listeners time to write down the one-two-three. But, all in all, it was great fun. We had quite a team: Des Lynam, Jim Rosenthal, Chris Rea, Christopher Martin-Jenkins, John Motson, Alan Parry and the late Peter Jones were all there throughout the seventies. We have nearly all gone to work full-time in our specialist disciplines, which is a great tribute to the grounding we received. It was very hard to leave and join the ITV network in 1981. A. P. 'Slim' Wilkinson, then head of sport, didn't want me to go, but I had always wanted to work in racing and this was my big chance. I was right, too, as it led to a job with Channel 4.

In those radio days, January was one of the busiest months for all sport. Still is. Luckily, the racing year for Channel 4 begins at Cheltenham. With the month packed full of quality generally – the FA Cup third round and the rugby union five-nations tournament are just two of the major events – we need top-notch racing to attract a good audience for the programme, setting us up for the rest of the month and year. It is highly competitive at this time: I can remember covering jumps racing at Ascot in January for Radio 2 and finding myself limited to the shortest of reports throughout the afternoon and in the sports report at five p.m. for a good National Hunt card. In January, even a top race like the Victor Chandler Chase at Ascot struggles to compete for air-time when it's up against a big FA Cup game. If racing cannot deliver some real excitement on the opening day of the new year, it may find it difficult to hang on to a reasonable audience for the next twelve months. Cheltenham, fortunately, is capable of setting a really up-beat tone.

Racing has a huge following. It is immensely popular, especially with footballers, as well as with plenty of other sports competitors, too. Mick Channon, the former England and Southampton player, is now an excellent trainer, and Kevin Keegan is heavily involved as a breeder of thoroughbreds. But it is worth remembering that racing is not in such great demand on television as some other sports, so we have to work really hard to keep our audience levels up. Just consider how much money Sky television pays the Premier League and Football League for rights to broadcast games live – hundred of millions compared to the few million racing receives for its media rights. Racing is a small part of today's very big sporting world, so it's a good thing that racing begins the year on television with a strong programme from the home of National Hunt racing. The great thing about starting at Cheltenham is that we can look forward to the Festival in three months' time. There are two Cheltenham meetings in January, both of which are covered by Channel 4. The question at the beginning and the end of the month after both of these fixtures has to be: what chance do these winners have of repeating their success in the middle of March at the very track from which we are broadcasting? January is the start of the build-up to the Festival and for many punters, either at the racecourse or watching on television, at this time of year only the Festival matters. Not even the Grand National enters their thoughts.

The first January meeting at Cheltenham is more of a holiday occasion than the second fixture of the month. But by the time January is drawing to a close and we find ourselves back at Cheltenham after excursions to the likes of Kempton and Sandown – weather permitting, of course – the programme is altogether more serious. It is all about unearthing a horse who stays on up the hill, and identifying stables that are running into form. The message that the regular viewers want to hear from the trainers and jockeys interviewed on Channel 4 is that a horse who has just won or run a great race will win again at the Festival. Channel 4 racing always aims to entertain all its audience, from hardened gambler to first-time viewer, but in January it's serious racing business and the search for the Festival 'banker' bet is on.

Cheltenham winners may emerge away from the racecourse in January, too, and at big ante-post odds. Alderbrook, who was trained by Kim Bailey to win the Champion Hurdle in 1995, was recommended to me by none other than Walter Swinburn, the flat-race jockey, after he partnered the top-notch performer on the level in a gallop for Julie Cecil, who trained the horse in the summer. It was late January when I received the nod, the horse had even run over hurdles, which meant I was on at 33–1 before Alderbrook won at Wincanton and showed everyone that he was good enough to win at Cheltenham.

I'm always on the lookout for a fancy-priced winner for the Festival around this time, but I'm not interested in a tip that is short odds and will mean that I have to wager a lot to make a lot. Without even knowing it Bob Champion put me off serious big betting for life. During his days as a jumps jockey, he rang me up with a tip for a runner he was partnering in a novice chase at Newbury. He really fancied it and in those days that was enough for me. I laid what for me was a big bet and settled back to watch the race, nice and relaxed, expecting to be considerably richer in a short space of time. The horse won, but only by the narrowest of margins – a head – getting up to beat the leaders on the line. Champ had been fourth jumping the last and he crawled over that fence. I was sure he was beaten. The last hundred yards took years off my life as he closed in on the front runners, and since then I have never bet more than I can reasonably afford to lose, and only a few times a year. I can do without the added stress. Maximum bet a monkey (£500), tops, maybe only two or three times a year, but that's the absolute limit.

Apart from the odd gem like Alderbrook, you'll struggle to hear a good tip from Newmarket in winter. During January the place is like a ghost town. My flat in Newmarket is at the bottom of Warren Hill and its gallops and in January I can look out of a window in the morning and hardly see a horse. In summer, it's like a busy motorway junction.

There is plenty going on, though, but not much on the gallops. Most preparations for the new flat-racing season are taking place behind stable doors: young horses being broken in ready for racing, older horses swimming to protect those ageing joints for another campaign, tactics being planned for big races ahead. You will see the odd personality about – Mick Ryan, the local trainer, riding around on his bicycle, or Don Cantona, an eccentric Irishman who rides his steeplechaser with a loyal Jack Russell on his lap. But you won't see a big trainer – Michael Stoute or Luca Cumani, and certainly not Henry Cecil – exercising a horse who is being aimed at the Classic races of the spring and summer. Only the all-weather gallops are open. The grass gallops, which a trainer preparing a horse for the 1000 or 2000 Guineas at Newmarket on the Rowley Mile racecourse would need to use, are not open until later in the year. The future stars are still largely wrapped in cotton wool. In January, the likes of Clive Brittain enjoy a lie-in: Newmarket's earliest riser who rides out four lots before racing – Dracula, because he works in the dark – is absent for the first few sunrises of the new year. Even trainers like Michael Bell or David Loder, who both like to have their horses fit and ready to run for the first day of the flat season at Doncaster in March, are quiet in January.

Trainers take the chance to go away but, like successful businessmen in other walks of life, Newmarket's biggest trainers – the town's backbone – are never really on holiday. In January, many go to Dubai, which is in the middle of its racing season. Sheikh Mohammed's Godolphin string, which winters in Dubai and races in Europe in the summer, is being prepared for a new season and a few rival camps like to check out the competition! For many, it is more of a busman's holiday. I remember settling down next to Ben Hanbury, who trained Midway Lady to win the 1000 Guineas and the Oaks at Epsom, on the beach in anticipation of a relaxing few hours in the sun only for him to produce a mobile phone and a stack of business cards. They kept him busy for over two hours, phoning owners, old and new, and bloodstock agents with interested clients.

I try to have a holiday around this time but I never manage it. Julie is always encouraging me to take time off as we need the rest. One of the problems is deciding where to go. These days I am quite a recognizable face to racing people, and occasionally I'm spotted by television viewers, especially those who get up in time for *The Morning Line*, which has a loyal following, and this can defeat the point of going away for a break. I was swimming off the beach in St Lucia one year when a head popped up, with mask and snorkel, to say hello, which was something of a surprise. That is why I like to go to Dubai for breaks, with Julie hopefully. I am there, anyway, to cover the racing at Nad Al Sheba, and with so many *really* famous racing people out there in January, no one is going to take any notice of me!

At home in Newmarket, I aim to jog every day to try to stay relaxed, but never manage it. I'm also a member of the Bedford Lodge Health Club. It has a swimming pool and aerobics classes, and I usually fit in a regular workout around the month's racing commitments. When I was a young lad I used to love all sport – I've tried everything – and I do like to try to stay in shape. Even when I'm working, I'm on the move and, if I make it a brisk pace, it all helps to keep me trim.

In my book real relaxation is spending time with Julie and friends. For me, they don't come any better than Bob Champion. Champ is like a brother to me. We talk every day and give each other advice when facing difficult decisions. We're shared some traumatic times since we first met more than forty years ago in Cleveland, and I hope to share a good few more evenings with him round the dinner table.

Bob's story is, of course, well known. He fought and beat cancer, and came back to ride the winner of the 1981 Grand National, Aldaniti, who had also made a miraculous recovery from injury. I remember what happened a year or so before that so well. Bob

[14]

had been in America riding and returned to England to have a lump – discovered by a female vet! – checked out by doctors. I was covering the Horse of the Year Show when he got the results confirming he had cancer. I was staying on the eighth floor of a London hotel. Bob told me he wanted to jump out of my window.

I remember going to see him at the Royal Marsden Hospital where he was being treated. He became so weak, so quickly. In only three months he went from being one of the fittest people I knew to wasting away. I would sit by his bed talking to him while he threw up as the drugs took effect. Once, after leaving him in the ward, I cried in the car park. I was sure that it was the last time I was going to see him alive. But Champ proved me wrong. They made a film about it – *Champions* – and you wouldn't believe the storyline if it wasn't based on real life.

Bob's cancer charity – the Bob Champion Cancer Trust – has raised millions and it is a measure of the man that although raising the money has probably interfered with his career as a trainer and his personal life he still believes it has all been worthwhile. That doesn't surprise me.

Champ was there for me after I met Julie and when my previous marriage was breaking up. I moved in with him then and we lived together for three years, during which time I got my life back together. I think we'll always be best mates.

Champ, and other friends, are a constant feature throughout my racing year, wherever events and commitments take me. I'm lucky to be involved in a sport that keeps me in touch with people I value and whom I have known for nearly my whole life. January is the start of twelve months' racing that covers Britain, Europe and the rest of the world. It will be hectic –

Morning Line, afternoons on air, racecourse commentating, and off-air promotional work to fill the gaps. And, hopefully, a lot of fun at the races, on the gallops, and in the company of some of the nicest people I know in racing.

FEBRUARY

Teamwork

Success in racing is always based on teamwork. The
best trainers make sure that they surround themselves with quality staff – a good head lad and travelling lad, top work riders, skilled vets and a reliable
stable jockey, or the best rider available for the racecourse end of the business. Working in television is no
different. I'm part of a great Channel 4 team made up
of people who all have a role to play in providing the
viewers with an exciting, smooth-running, stimulating
programme. Unless we work as a team, it doesn't work
at all.

At a racecourse like, say, Sandown in February,
everyone is spread all over the track, ensuring that
every aspect of the day's racing is brought to viewers
at home. I'm usually with Brough Scott in the winner's
enclosure, which is behind the grandstand and the
paddock, in front of the jockeys' weighing room. John
Francome and Jim McGrath – or maybe a combination
from John Oaksey, Alastair Down and Lesley Graham
– are positioned to view the runners in the paddock
and the field going down to post for the start, while
John McCririck is playing his usual role among the

betting public to report changes in the odds as they happen. Of course, there's also Graham Goode, or maybe Simon Holt if he's not reading the results as they come in from around the country. One of them will be in the commentary box to see the runners make their way to the start and finally to call them home.

Andrew Franklin holds the whole team together, helped by Jane Garrod, the director of Channel 4 racing. Andrew is the producer: that means he has everyone's microphone linked to his earpiece. He has talk-back from as many as ten people at once and while this is going on he has to consider which picture we should be screening from the ten cameras in service on an average Channel 4 race day. Getting all that to gel is a great skill.

Andrew should be an inspiration to anyone with ambitions to succeed in television. His father was a farmer and there is no television experience in the family. As a young man, he simply wrote to ITV's *World of Sport*, featuring, of course, the ITV Seven, got a job as a tea-boy and ended up editing that programme before moving to racing on Channel 4 when *World of Sport* went off air. He is living proof that you can make it all the way up from the bottom. Andrew is the driving force behind the racing coverage on Channel 4. His commitment is complete. He doesn't drink much, and when we're working he can survive on the minimum of sleep. He's obsessive, a perfectionist, and the best television producer with whom I have ever worked. He also has great ideas about racing and other sports, and is a brilliant innovator.

During an afternoon broadcast, Andrew's job is to focus on the achievements of the day and also to look ahead to the forthcoming racing scheduled for Channel 4's future afternoon programmes. Everything is geared towards celebrating the afternoon's highlights and considering how the performances of the day affect the rest of the season's high spots, the Classics, Newmarket, Epsom, Doncaster, and forthcoming races at places like York on the flat and, of course, Cheltenham and the Festival over jumps.

In February, the efforts of every horse running, especially those Champion Hurdle and Gold Cup contenders who are taking part in the month's many two-mile hurdle races and staying chases, are considered with the Festival in mind.

Sandown's February meeting at the beginning of the month is a key fixture, with Cheltenham so close. The programmes broadcast from Esher in February, like the ones from Cheltenham in January, are full of Festival thoughts. Sandown is particularly relevant to the Festival. Sandown's finish is up a steep hill, as is Cheltenham's, so I am hoping to hear from owners, trainers and jockeys if their horses have finished tired or fresh, if the race has put them spot on for Cheltenham and if they can be expected to show some improvement next time out in March.

But I try to be careful not to go too overboard about the Cheltenham significance of a performance at Sandown. The hill finish means its usually a big-hearted horse who wins – exactly what you need for Cheltenham – but trainers have to be careful that they don't end up jeopardizing their chances of a win at the Festival by asking too much of a stable star too early in the year. You can, as they say, leave your chances of winning at Cheltenham at the top of Sandown's hill. The dilemma is that most Sandown races are worth winning in their own right. I'd hate to be the trainer of the Cheltenham Gold Cup favourite with the job of having the horse spot on for that big day in March and also the chance of winning at Sandown the month before.

Sandown is a fair track, where the best usually wins, but it has a number of unique features. It is a home for track specialists – like Desert Orchid and, from a few years earlier, the brilliant Tingle Creek – with its Railway Fences on the far side away from the grandstand. These three fences close together allow a horse very little time to recover from even a minor jumping error. Then there is the Pond Fence up the hill, which takes some jumping, and, of course, the Sandown hill itself, a real climb. Horses who win time and time again at Sandown may not enjoy the same success elsewhere as this track's demands are not made of horses at other racecourses.

That said, winning on the day is what racing is all about. Success for a course specialist can make a Saturday at Sandown a real treat, regardless of how it affects the Cheltenham picture. It's a great Saturday course for me and the atmosphere hums if an old favourite, maybe trained by a local, lands a big prize at a nice price for regular punters on the main sporting day of the week. If it's one of Sandown's magic moments, racing can make the afternoon's main sporting headline – whatever the football thrills on the same Saturday.

It's a long day. Hard work. *The Morning Line* is an early start and I have to be on the ball for the whole afternoon. I like to round things off with a quiet evening having dinner in the Plough, always a popular spot for Newmarket's racing folk. If there has been some success for a Sandown regular with a big local following, the evening meal is all the more enjoyable and the effort worthwhile – even two hours in the Sandown wind and rain. It also makes great television.

Sandown always makes me think of Brough's career as a jockey. My father took me racing there a long time ago and, although I can't remember which year it was,

I remember Brough as an amateur riding a winner there in the late sixties. Today, he calls me Big Fella. The name comes from a piece I did about a horse trained by Jack Ormston in the fifties, called Le Garcon D'Or, who had a race named after him. During the interview, I said, 'Hello, big fella,' to the horse, who was no more than fifteen hands, which is pretty small for a fully grown thoroughbred. The name has stuck – at least with Brough.

Brough went into television before me. He says he had no choice, really, as it was all there was left for him to do after riding – to write and talk, that's all. Brough is one of the hardest workers I know. I remember him arriving just in the nick of time one day in the early eighties for a broadcast at Ayr. I expected an excuse for his time-keeping, based on something along the lines of frozen points at Watford, but he told me he'd been in Dubai – as it transpired later to arrange the setting up of the *Racing Post*, the Maktoum-owned daily racing paper. All this was a long time before Dubai became such a significant part of the racing world. It took me by surprise but, of course, today it would hardly raise a comment. But that is Brough for you. Always ahead of the game. He is a tireless worker for charity, and is unassuming about it and all his other achievements. He has run marathons to raise money for worthy causes and completed the sixty miles of the Lyke Wake Walk with the racing reporter Tim Richards, John Oaksey, and Andrew Franklin. My father gave him a book about this trek across the Cleveland Hills and that was all the inspiration Brough needed. A modest man, a great colleague and also a good friend.

Jim McGrath – Jimbo to everyone now, but I don't think he really likes his nickname – used to be the serious member of the Channel 4 racing team, but working with John Francome has relaxed him no end. He also works for *Timeform*, the company that sells its own racecards and notebooks with ratings for runners included. *Timeform* takes its racing seriously, but Jim is better now. A specialist in dirty jokes, these days, and a useful man to have in your pub quiz team!

Jim is involved in racing right the way through. He has shares in a lot of horses spread across the country with lots of different trainers, breeds from his own mares, and really loves the game. He is friends with some of the most astute brains in racing, including trainers, owners, jockeys, breeders and bookmakers. He's also a bit of a punter. I remember a day at Ayr when Jim described a race finish – 'the winner did it nicely in the end' – and then, cool as you like, put his hand over the microphone to tell us that he had just won £20,000 on the result. He's very generous with it. He gave my two sons, Alex and James, ten pounds each for a bet on their first day at the races and always gives the Channel 4 girls a tenner for a bet on the Epsom Derby. A great professional with a kind heart.

It's interesting the way that John Francome has changed Jim. Franks has that effect on people: when you're feeling down, he is the one person I know who is guaranteed to pick you up. He can seem a hard, sometimes cold, racing man, possibly because he was a jockey – one of the greats, mind you – exposed to the business side of the game, but his ability to cheer a place up is unbelievable. He's almost better at it than he was at riding and that's saying something! John is also a great businessman. He devours the *Financial Times* before breakfast and didn't need to borrow a penny when he built his house, which is situated on three hundred beautiful acres. I'd love to live in his garage.

John has everything, looks, talent, wit, and a wicked

sense of humour. We once did a theatre tour together, along with Champ and Steve Smith-Eccles, entitled *That's Racing*. On the first night, in Southport, John suggested that I open the show by asking him what he had for breakfast that morning. He said he had a funny answer to get things rolling. Well, on the night he answered simply, 'Cornflakes.' I was speechless. He got me then and he's been getting me ever since. What's more, as well as stitching me up time and time again, he's always thinking about the money side of a venture. The *That's Racing* show was a classic example. Before the opening night, Franks asked me why we were hosting the show at Southport, on the coast, as it meant that people would be able to come only from three sides. Always on the ball where money's concerned, that's Franks.

Of course, no discussion of the Channel 4 line-up would be complete without mention of John McCririck. Big Mac is Mac. I have known him and worked with him for a long time and he's a great professional. The great thing about working with him is that you can always look to him for a comment or some aside – especially on *The Morning Line*. When I'm in the middle of an item or interview that's not going brilliantly, I can pop it over to Mac for his input, live on air, and it will always come back possessing something with which I can work.

Mac has changed over the years. There is less of the private side to him, these days. He's in so much demand and is always expected to be the larger-than-life master of the betting ring at the racecourse that he is on Channel 4. Today, the real John is a rare sight. He's what the public wants him to be and it's almost impossible to have a quiet dinner with him as he's always being interrupted by admirers and critics. By the dessert course, I sometimes feel like joining some

[23]

of the viewers of an afternoon's racing on Channel 4 whom Mac has annoyed and turning him off! But he's brilliant at what he does, make no mistake. His book-making information is second to none and the statistics he provides before a race on winning favourites and the like are invaluable. He also has a great eye for a line in the newspapers on all sports, which he devours like his food. He reviews the Saturday papers on *The Morning Line* and comes up with some great quotes. The only loser out of all this is his wife, whom he calls the Boobie. She has to go out at night to collect the first editions so that he can read them when he wakes at six a.m. the following morning and be ready for *The Morning Line* at nine. A long-suffering lady!

John McCririck will tell you that his finest moment came when all the microphones went dead while we were on air at Doncaster and Andrew told him through his earpiece that he was the only presenter with a voice. It was the highlight of his life. 'I'm in total control!' he screamed. The reverse was true when he incurred the wrath of Michael Grade, who was then head of Channel 4 and therefore our ultimate boss. Mac was reviewing the papers on *The Morning Line* and took an especially hard line against Manchester's bid for the 2000 Olympics. 'It's always raining there,' he moaned. Just after we went off air the phone rang and it was Michael wanting to tell John that, as the boss of Channel 4, he was also one of the key figures behind Manchester's efforts to win the right to stage the Games. The colour drained from Mac's cheeks. I think he was more cautious in criticizing Manchester's weather after that.

My escape from Big Mac in February – in fact, from November to April – is Dubai, where things are begin-ning to build up to the climax of the Dubai World Cup at the end of March. I spend a lot of the month shuttling back and forth to and from Dubai. It provides quite a contrast: the green turf of Sandown in February and huge seventeen-hand steeplechasers, against the sand track of Nad Al Sheba racecourse and perfectly proportioned flat bred thoroughbreds. The rain, sleet and even snow of Britain, and the arid heat of Dubai. I have two completely different wardrobes, one for the warm in Dubai and one for the wet of a British winter.

The first time I visited Dubai was in 1994 for the first international jockey's challenge that was staged there. I got involved with the commentary at Nad Al Sheba because I had the courage to ask before anyone else and Sheikh Mohammed liked the idea. Sheikh Mohammed, the central figure behind the development of Dubai as a racing centre as well as one of the world's most powerful racehorse owners, was at York so I went up to the private room he has there to talk to him about my possible involvement. I was quite nervous. I walked into the room and the Sheikh stood up, which meant everyone else had to! But after that, I sat down next to him and I was given a chance to explain what I felt I could bring to the racing in Dubai. He told me to sort out everything with his team. Up to then, there had been no real racecourse commentaries, apart from those by Pat Buckley, the Grand National winning jockey, who did the job at nearby Abu Dhabi. It was a great honour to land the work.

I remember the first time I went to Dalham Hall, the nerve centre of Sheikh Mohammed's Darley Stud Management racing and breeding operation in Newmarket. I was with Bill Smith, the retired National Hunt jockey who now works for the BBC's National Hunt racing team and also acts as an adviser to Sheikh Mohammed's brother, Sheikh Hamdan. I left my car but then realized I hadn't locked it and returned to secure the doors. All this prompted Bill to ask me exactly whom I was expecting to drive off with it, considering the choice! Of the vehicles parked, mine was the last one that would be pinched.

I cope with the demands of the February workload, with all its contrasts in climate and culture, by sticking to a routine. I remember reading about the great television presenter David Frost, who used to commute between New York and London and work at both ends of his journey. I have tried to follow his example: I don't drink much on the plane, and try to sleep. The time difference means that I can fly out from Heathrow at 8 p.m. and arrive in Dubai at 7 a.m., returning on a flight that takes off after racing in the evening and arrives in the morning. If I'm lucky, my body clock doesn't notice the change. When I arrive in Dubai, a car is waiting at the airport to take me to the hotel, and we go via the racecourse where I pick up a copy of *Al-Adiyat*, the Gulf's *Sporting Life*. After a short nap and a freshen-up, I'm at the track. Mark Monkhouse is waiting for me there. His father-in-law is Paddy Rudkin, formerly head lad to Henry Cecil and now a trainer in Dubai. Mark updates me on all the news and gossip and any changes to the statistics for owners, jockeys and trainers since the last meeting. There is also the racecard to study. These are produced by Khalifa Bin Dasmal, who owned Shaamit, the 1996 Epsom Derby winner, and who is also a member of the Dubai Racing Committee. After all the homework, everything is ready for an excellent evening's racing.

You have to go to Dubai to appreciate exactly what the Maktoum family has achieved in establishing it as a major racing centre. The track at Nad Al Sheba is a state-of-the-art design with excellent spectator comforts. The stable barns have been built with the needs of the modern trainer and thoroughbred in mind. New stables can be built in only four weeks and the racecourse grandstand was expanded simply by lifting off the roof, building an extra floor, and putting it back on again. Initially, the racing authorities in Dubai had to go to great lengths to satisfy the international regulations for the quarantine of racehorses, but now a horse has to spend hardly any time in isolation before it is allowed to exercise on the track and run in races. There is also a veterinary hospital which, under the supervision of Mike 'The Doc' Hauser, has acquired an international reputation for excellence. The post-race dope-testing facilities are the envy of world racing. Security is so tight that even Prince Fahd Salman was not allowed in when he was being shown around the racing complex by Sheikh Mohammed. The development has put Dubai on the world map in no uncertain terms.

The Godolphin experiment, along with the inaugural Dubai World Cup in 1996, took Dubai on to an even higher plane. Sheikh Mohammed – the boss, as everyone calls him – was behind the Godolphin idea of taking horses out of Europe during the close season and wintering them in the warmer climate of Dubai. The project began in 1993 with a few horses, and by 1997 the Godolphin string, under the supervision of Saeed Bin Suroor, numbered 125 horses and had numerous Classic wins – Moonshell and Balanchine's Epsom Oaks, Mark of Esteem's 2000 Guineas – to its name as well as a host of other big races. During February, the horses are being prepared for a European campaign and times are kept of all the gallops they do on the dirt at Nad Al Sheba. But fitness is not the only goal: they are all also taught how to settle in races and about the demands of competitive racing. If you see the care and attention that goes into preparing Godolphin's horses you aren't surprised by the success they have enjoyed in such a short time.

Like Channel 4, Godolphin is a team effort from top to bottom with everyone working flat out for months on end. Saeed is attending to horses for what seems like twenty-four hours a day, helped by Tommy Albertrani, his assistant who used to work for the big American Bill Mott, trainer of the mighty Cigar.

Simon Crisford is Godolphin's general manager. If Saeed works twenty-four hours a day, Simon works twenty-five. He served as assistant to a number of top trainers – Sir Mark Prescott for one – before taking a job as Newmarket correspondent for the *Racing Post*. Now, he can be in his office in Dubai and there will be a queue of ten people all waiting to see him on urgent matters. Those who work with him share his drive to be the best. Simon has a keen sense of fun, too. I remember going to see Sheikh Mohammed and finding him deep in conversation about running yearlings, who had wintered in Dubai, at Royal Ascot as two-year-olds. When I was asked for my opinion, I suggested that they run a few, just to dip the toe in the water, and see how the horses performed. It was a success: one winner from three runners. After Ascot, when I caught up with the boss at Newmarket to congratulate him and Simon's team, Simon, who also joined us, said that he was glad he had persuaded us both in the end to run the horses.

With Simon and the team's help, Sheikh Mohammed has taken Godolphin to the top of the world training tree. But Dubai today is not just about horses. It is also home to a dry dock, one of two man-made constructions – the other is the Great Wall of China – which can be seen from the moon. The Dubai sea port is the busiest in the world and there is a thriving international business community. Also on the sporting front, there is a great golf course where a European professional tour event takes place every year, tennis and snooker tournaments, and water sports championships, all world-class standard. Not bad for a country that is no more than twenty-five years old.

With all the flying I do, February is the beginning of a crazy time for me. The comforts of Dubai and the welcome I receive make the travel and long hours bearable. And February is an exciting time. The adrenaline is beginning to flow, too, and this helps with the workload. The star performers of the new flat season are limbering up, there is the Dubai World Cup, Cheltenham, the Grand National and, ahead, a summer of excellence on the level. It is a time of great expectations and optimism. February's contrasts of climate and time zone can cause me some confusion when I wake up first thing and wonder in which country I have been sleeping, but the variety keeps my mind fresh. I love it.

MARCH

Festival Times

The three days of the Cheltenham National Hunt Festival usually fall around the middle of March, but the occasion dominates the entire month. In fact, all our Channel 4 coverage of National Hunt racing in the year so far will have been geared towards the three days of the Cheltenham Festival. The closer the meeting's opening day comes, the greater the sense of anticipation, right up to when the starter lets the runners go for the first race on the Tuesday afternoon.

If you're a racing fan you can't argue with this or, indeed, the way that we on Channel 4 make Cheltenham the focus of all our programmes and broadcasts from January onwards. The quality of the jumps racing for those three days at Prestbury Park in March is second to none and rarely disappoints. Each of the three days is brimful of the best National Hunt horses in training, bidding for championship events or running in highly competitive handicaps. From the racegoer's point of view it's an unbeatable three days of sport. Professionally speaking, it's great, too: every winner has a story to tell.

Channel 4 won the contract to cover Cheltenham's

racing all year round, including the Festival. It was a great coup for us. When the news was finally confirmed, everyone on the team was thrilled.

There were a few more butterflies than normal floating around in the stomachs of the Channel 4 team for our first broadcast from Prestbury Park. Over the years BBC had covered the racing from Cheltenham so well and we knew that everyone in racing would be watching to make sure that Channel 4 maintained the standard.

I think the point to bear in mind when considering the respective merits of the two stations is that we on Channel 4 have always looked to take a few risks and experiment with different ideas. Inevitably some of these ideas don't always work and they are scrapped, but if an innovation catches on then we have enhanced the whole programme's content. Who knows? The BBC might take our ideas on board a bit later. If you compare Channel 4 to a football team, we are more like Kevin Keegan's Newcastle United than George Graham's Leeds. We play an attacking game and take a few chances coming forward, which means we score some great goals but also let a few in at the back.

I felt that our style of coverage at Cheltenham was vindicated when Jane Garrod and Andrew Franklin were nominated for a BAFTA award for the coverage of Thursday's Gold Cup. Jane, as director, had to handle twenty or so cameras, which meant we were able to show new angles of the racing and carry more interviews and features than ever before.

For me, covering the Festival for television capped a lifetime of great personal Cheltenham memories, stretching all the way back to the days of working for Denys Smith at Bishop Auckland and riding in point-to-points. I never made it round Cheltenham in the saddle – it's a professional's course – but as a racegoer,

I have seen great horses run there, including Arkle, maybe the greatest of them all. I led horses up to Cheltenham, in my teenage years, although not, I'm sorry to say, at the Festival itself. These were great times, full of funny moments. At one of Cheltenham's meetings I had to stay overnight in the stable lads' hostel. Everyone was fast asleep when suddenly the lights went on in the middle of the night and a voice announced, 'I'm back.' It was a lad from Ireland who had travelled over with the brilliant two-mile chaser, Flyingbolt. I think it's fair to say that the lad was a little the worse for wear. No one seemed to mind that he had woken us up just to say that he had got back from the pub!

I started working for radio at the Cheltenham Festival in 1972, so 1997 was my twenty-fifth anniversary of broadcasting from there. Back in the early seventies, Bob Champion lived in Hungerford. I was staying with him and I would try to ride out to Lambourn with one of the local trainers before driving to the track. It didn't always work out like that. One year we stayed late at the racecourse and went on afterwards in to the town and didn't get back to Hungerford until the early hours of the morning. On arriving, I picked up a message from Champ's Ansaphone telling me that the bulletins for the breakfast news were scheduled to be live from the track, beginning at six a.m. Bob and I decided the best thing to do was turn straight round. We got back to Cheltenham just after five and I went live at six. Bob stayed in the car, asleep, and poetic licence got the better of me: on air I said that we had been walking the course and that jockey Bob Champion felt that the ground was raceable after the night's frost. Later in the day, Major Derek Wigan, the trainer for whom Bob was riding at the time, commended him for his attention to detail and great professionalism! If only he had known.

Cheltenham then had an altogether different style and atmosphere from today's high pressure, slick, modern, corporate Festival. There was a bar at the bottom of the old grandstand where everyone – all the big names, the Biddlecombes, the Carberrys – would cram in for a drink after racing and sometimes before. Champagne was only about a fiver a bottle. Nowadays, for me, it's a lot of hard work, and after three days of it, rounding off with the Cheltenham Gold Cup on Thursday, I'm finished. A *Morning Line* goes out every day, which means I have to peak twice in eight hours. The Channel 4 team meeting for the afternoon programme begins at nine forty-five a.m., almost straight after *The Morning Line* finishes. It helps me to do *The Morning Line* because it means I've done a lot of the preparation for the afternoon well in advance. The Festival is three full days. I am wiped out by Thursday night when it is all over. Sad, but a little relieved that there is no *Morning Line* on Friday.

During the eighties, when I was working for ITV, and Channel 4 before we won the contract, I missed some of the great moments live of the Cheltenham Festivals. My schedule meant that I was often covering something else or preparing for the weekend's Saturday ITV Seven and sometimes absent for all three days. I was not there for Dawn Run's tremendous success in the Gold Cup in 1986. For me that was Peter O'Sullevan's finest hour at the microphone – 'The mare is going to get up' – and the career highlight for Jonjo O'Neill, another jockey, like Champ, who has won the battle against cancer. Jonjo is one of the nicest guys in racing. Everyone wishes him well. But even if I missed out on a few truly great Festival thrills, I still have a stack of memories, even if some of them were only as a television viewer or radio listener.

One of my most vivid recollections is of Michael Dickinson having trained the first five home in the 1983 Gold Cup. I remember someone saying at the time that it would have been better for horses from the same stable as the winner and placed two to five to have tried to win other races. I agree, to some extent, as horses like Wayward Lad and Captain John, who finished behind the Gold Cup winner, Bregawn, were good enough to beat the best of the rest on their day. But you never know how things are going to work out in jumps racing. An odds-on favourite can fall at the first and Bregawn was only 100–30 with the bookmakers. You have to take your chance. After all, it's the Gold Cup. Whatever your thoughts on Michael's strategy, to train the first five home in the Gold Cup was, and remains, an unbelievable achievement. I don't think it will ever be repeated.

Knowing Michael, as I do, he probably celebrated with half a glass of champagne at the most. He came to my twenty-first birthday party when we both lived in Yorkshire and certainly enjoyed himself then, but he has always worried about his weight. We rode together as amateurs and, at over six foot, Michael had to waste away or spend hours in the sauna. Even on such a special occasion as training the first five in the Gold Cup he would never let himself go. Old habits die hard. I reckon that he could have been champion National Hunt trainer for fifteen years if he had stayed in the jumping game – he seemed to be streets ahead of his rivals at the time – but he fancied a crack at the flat. Robert Sangster offered him the opportunity to work as a private trainer at Manton, which was just too good to turn down. It's a pity that things didn't work out for either Robert, the new owner, or Michael, who was sacked in effect after a season of very few winners.

Perhaps Michael just didn't have the right tempera-
ment for the job of restoring Manton – historically, one
of the great training establishments in British racing –
to its former glories. He may have spent too much time
working on re-establishing the turf quality of the gallops instead of concentrating on registering a few winners for the new boss. Barry Hills, who replaced him,
certainly benefited from all Michael's hard work, and
Michael has proved since then that he can train a big
winner on the flat. Since he moved to America, he has
saddled plenty of decent horses, including a Breeders'
Cup winner.

Michael was never one of the great 'characters' of
the Festival: his personality is quite subdued. Even
when he had a really big Festival winner he seemed
almost automated in radio interviews I did with him
after the race. Always in control. His mother, Mrs
Monica Dickinson, is altogether different: she is a fixture at the Festival, and a great traditionalist. Channel
4 was not popular in the Dickinson household when
we introduced horseback interviews with winning
jockeys at Cheltenham in 1997. Mrs Dickinson wrote to
the *Sporting Life* the week after Lesley Graham had
interviewed a winning jockey at Cheltenham on
horseback for the first time: she was not happy, believ-
ing that a jockey should talk to trainer and owner first.

Brod Munro-Wilson, the former jockey, is one of the
less well-known Cheltenham personalities associated
with Prestbury Park and the Festival, but he won the
Foxhunters and sticks in my mind. One year he rode a
winner I backed and the Tote didn't have enough cash
on the day to pay out everyone. It hardly mattered that
Brod's finish was one of the worst demonstrations of
race riding up the Cheltenham hill I think I have ever
seen! He was all over the place. But he still won and
that's the main thing.

Steve Smith-Eccles was a bit more stylish in the saddle, and contributed his fair share of stories out of it to the Cheltenham legend. During the eighties he had a brilliant association with the Champion Hurdler See You Then and together they won a hat-trick of hurdling crowns. Nicky Henderson, See You Then's trainer, performed miracles in getting the horse, who had bad knee joints, to the Festival, let alone winning the race three times in a row. See You Then was one of the Cheltenham greats with the heart of a lion.

As all racing fans know, John Francome would have ridden See You Then in his first Champion Hurdle, but Franks had a bad fall in the race before and missed what would have developed into a great association. Mind you, Franks has a hatful of Cheltenham memories, including a win in the Champion Hurdle on Sea Pigeon in 1981, and a Gold Cup success on Midnight Court in 1978. As a jockey, Franks had the best hands of any horseman I have ever seen, apart from Eddie Macken, the Irish show jumper, whom I saw ride when I was commentating on equestrian events like the Horse of the Year Show and the Royal International Horse Show. Franks would always just slip into the saddle and with just a gentle touch of the reins put the horse completely at ease. What a rapport. A real gift.

Of course, it's the Irish who make the Festival the truly great occasion it is today. They bring across the water the atmosphere that makes Cheltenham probably the best three days' racing of the year. Like everyone else involved with racing, anywhere in the world, I love the Irish and the fun they bring to the game, and especially to Cheltenham. They have been on hand over the years to salute 'home' wins by the likes of Danoli in a way that no other nation could match. The Irish take their racing seriously, too: I've done a piece for Irish radio every Saturday for the last twenty years and racing is always featured early in the broadcast, no matter what else is happening that day.

But perhaps more than anything the Irish love the Festival, and their affection for the event and their optimistic outlook were summed up for me by an interview I did on the Saturday before Cheltenham in 1996. Andrew Franklin had asked me to go to Cheltenham that day to film an item setting the scene for the following Tuesday and to be shown during that afternoon's broadcast from Sandown. I travelled down from opening a betting shop in Carlisle and arrived at the track at eight a.m. to interview the clerk of the course, Philip Arkwright, about the state of the ground, and was greeted by a friendly Irishman on board a strapping chaser. The horse was Imperial Call, so we did an interview next to the statue of Dawn Run. 'Mr Thompson, this horse will win the Gold Cup on Thursday,' said the lad. He was right.

We try to bring a bit of the Irish love of racing on to *The Morning Line* during Cheltenham in the shape of Ted Walsh, Irish racing's best pundit and a part-time trainer too. He has ridden winners at the Festival, and he trained Commanche Court, who won the Triumph Hurdle in 1997, which means he can speak with authority about what it takes to win one of jump racing's top prizes. In making his well-argued points, Ted never uses one word when twenty will do but has a real style of his own and knows both English and Irish form back to front. He speaks his mind. He was an uncompromising rider with the whip and doesn't hold back with his opinions when asked for them, even on air. This is great television but it can get quite heated, and it's my job to keep a balance, which is not always easy. Ted's foil at home is Robert Hall, who is rarely fazed. I think he was even quite calm the year he didn't have enough money to pay for his round of drinks at Annabelle's. In Ireland, he keeps everyone focused on the programme.

After all the excitement of Cheltenham, the start of the flat season at Doncaster in the second half of March can seem a bit of an anti-climax. A few years ago Doncaster certainly seemed to lack something but John Sanderson, the clerk of the course at Town Moor, has changed this and has built up the three days of racing, which traditionally kick off the new term. Some thought has been put into the idea of moving the fixture to after the Grand National at the beginning of April so that the great race doesn't suffocate the start of the Flat. There was certainly a case for this a few years ago, but less so since John took over. Some people think that the racing on the flat around this time of year is a bit 'Mickey Mouse', but there are always plenty of runners and it is good betting. Punters who don't bet on racing over jumps look forward to Doncaster in March with the same anticipation that jumps fans do Cheltenham. For them, the long winter is finally over.

The Lincoln, over a mile on the Saturday of Doncaster, is one of the great handicaps in British racing and is a good betting heat to get things started for the new year. Thursday's Brocklesby Stakes, the season's first two-year-old racing of the year, is a tricky one for picking a winner. Jack Berry, whose horses are always fit and ready to run on day one of the new year, thinks he'll win it every year, but you can pick up a tip for almost every runner in the field. That doesn't mean, though, that you can't make some money at the start of the flat if you back horses selectively. Just remember to close your ears when, for instance, someone says to you 'Michael Bell's got a real flying machine this year' or 'Jack's is a certainty in the Brocklesby', and you'll be fine.

I think it's nonsense to say that racing around this time is of a poor standard. People who say this aren't moving with the times. Look at the Dubai World Cup. Now, there's one of the biggest races of the flat season for British trainers in the first month of the new year. Anyone who was privileged to be at the first running of the Dubai World Cup in 1996 would acknowledge that the event seems sure to grow into one of the racing highlights of the year. For me the race, which was won by the great American champion dirt horse Cigar, was an unqualified success and reinforced Dubai's standing as one of the racing world's most important venues. In years to come, March could become the key month, and races like those on Breeders' Cup day will be preparing the world's best older horses for the challenge of a world championship in the desert a few months later.

I was lucky enough to have some insight into the planning for the first World Cup in 1996. I was in Dubai for the second International Jockeys' Challenge in 1995. When I am working at Nad Al Sheba I have to pass through the grandstand's royal box to get to and from the commentary position. On the night, Sheikh Mohammed was sitting alone, reading a pamphlet, which I later realized was the International Racing Bureau's feasibility study for the race. He looked up and asked me what distance I thought was best for an international race for older horses that would be the richest in the world. I said that if you put up a big enough purse and staged the race over ten furlongs you might attract both the milers and the twelve-furlong stayers. But I stressed that the purse would have to be too big for owners and trainers to ignore. Sheikh Mohammed showed me the page of the IRB feasibility study covering prize money, which suggested a purse of around $4 million. That was, as the boss said to me, a lot of noughts!

[39]

At a party in November – five months before the first World Cup – to celebrate the success Godolphin had enjoyed during the year's previous European season, I spoke again with Sheikh Mohammed about the race, which was by then very much a reality. We talked about Cigar. I felt strongly that the race needed the American champion: without him it would not really be able to call itself a World Cup. Then, Cigar was the undisputed champion of the world: he had just won the Breeders' Cup Classic and had smashed record after record in America. The race had to have him in the field or it would have been like a football World Cup without Brazil. Sheikh Mohammed told me not to worry. Cigar, he said, would come. You see, the boss knew something that I didn't. Allen Paulson, who owned Cigar, had made his millions in aviation. He is also a keen pilot and, during a round the world flight, he passed through Dubai to refuel before continuing on his journey. Apparently, the fuelling stop at Dubai's airport was the quickest anywhere in the world. The speed of the airport ground staff helped to persuade Paulson to run Cigar.

The week before the race the build-up to the inaugural World Cup was amazing: there was a concert by Simply Red, a gala dinner for connections, and a host of other events, like the draw for the race, which all turned into special occasions. We recorded interviews with some of the celebrity guests who were arriving for the big race on the Wednesday. There were all the big names in racing, and people like Imran Khan, the Pakistan cricketer who has gone into politics in his homeland, and Burt Bacharach, the singer, who stayed in the room next to Julie and me in the hotel.

On the night before the race, I hosted a phone-in programme on who would win the World Cup, with Clive Brittain, Brough Scott and Kevin 'Hunk' Greely, the racing secretary at the Dubai Racing Club, answering the questions. There was also a fax machine, and although the programme went well, the fax kept ringing without anything coming through. Brough was all for taking it off the hook, but then something began to appear from the machine: a print-out of all the faxes that had been sent that day. It was lucky that, with such a great field for the race headed by the mighty Cigar, there were plenty of talking points from all the phone calls or, lacking faxes, we might have had to struggle to keep the show interesting.

The race itself was a huge success, due to the efforts of, among others, Michael Osborne, chairman of the World Cup committee, and, of course, Brough, who worked tirelessly behind the scenes. In the months leading up to the race the weather had threatened to make things difficult for the organizers. The rains came in February, which tested the track's drainage to the limit and flooded the car parks. In the end, though, the sun shone for the week before the race, and it was a dazzling night on the Wednesday of the race. Cigar's performance capped it all. He won brilliantly from Soul of the Matter, owned by Burt Bacharach, our neighbour, whose singing in the bath had been a joy all week! It was a great honour for me to do the race-course commentary for the inaugural Dubai World Cup, which went out all over the world via satellite television.

Events like the World Cup are the future. I see that Michael Osborne is hoping to put together a World Thoroughbred Series of races running throughout the season and carrying a bonus of about $10 million for the horse who performs best over, say, eight races spread through the year. I'm sure that we will see more and more big dirt races for older horses all over the globe, drawing international fields. The Dubai

World Cup shows it can be achieved. Even the weather couldn't stop the second running of the World Cup: it was rained off on the Saturday but went ahead on the following Thursday with Singspiel's victory for Sheikh Mohammed a fitting reward for the lengths to which he has gone to establish the race as the flat-racing high-light of the month – and increasingly the international racing year. There will always be Cheltenham, but in future March should hold so much more for me – and you.

APRIL

National Interests

The Grand National has an amazing capacity to produce stories that touch, fascinate or thrill all followers of racing. There seems to be an out-of-the-ordinary tale to tell about every winner, year after year after year. The race, over four and a half miles, is a one-off so perhaps it is not surprising that it has produced so many incredible results and stories. It is the highlight of April and one of the high spots of the calendar, jumping and flat. Even 1997's Monday Grand National, when the Saturday running had to be abandoned after a bomb scare, produced a remarkable outcome with Lord Gyllene making every yard of the race in front of a 20,000 crowd set on defying those who had ruined the occasion forty-eight hours earlier.

Behind the scenes I was lucky enough to share a little of one of the great Grand National stories of all time: Bob Champion's win in 1981 on Aldaniti. Sadly, I was not there on the great day. I had joined ITV and the Grand National at Aintree has always been covered only by the BBC. But I managed to talk to Bob on the phone after the race to congratulate him and enjoy the inside story. Champ seemed more concerned to point out that I had made a few mistakes on television myself that afternoon, but I know how much it really meant to him. I think when I talked to him he had yet to take in exactly what he and Aldaniti had accomplished. Both of them were lucky to be alive, let alone in the winner's enclosure at Aintree after the Grand National.

The National has been a BBC television race since the first broadcast in 1960 when Merryman won, accompanied by the voice of Peter O'Sullevan. Since I moved to ITV I have had to make do with tuning in, along with millions of viewers who cannot make it to Aintree, but the quality of the BBC's broadcast has always been excellent. Peter has now commentated on fifty Grand Nationals, and many people reckon that his finest hour was his commentary in 1973 when Red Rum overhauled Crisp in that long Aintree run to the winning post after the last. Remember that Crisp, who was an Australian champion, carried top weight and had been in the lead for virtually the whole race. At one point on the second circuit, he was in front by a huge margin and seemed sure to run out the winner. But Peter Bromley was the first to spot that Crisp, ridden by Richard Pitman, was in trouble: he went from predicting that it was going to be one of the greatest victories in the National to screaming that defeat was staring Crisp in the face.

Crisp's defeat, captured so brilliantly by both Peters, and Red Rum's first Grand National win was my début as a radio commentator on the race. I can remember it so well. The commentary teams for radio and television are spread around the Aintree circuit – you need more than one commentator to cover the National – and I was due to pick up from the late Michael O'Hehir, the great Irish voice of racing. He handed over to me and my heart was beating almost

out of my chest. I think the first thing I said was something like, 'Three fences have fallen at that horse'! The
race was particularly exciting for me as Brian Fletcher,
who was still a good friend from the days I spent
working at Denys Smith's stable, was riding Red Rum
for Ginger McCain. Peter Bromley captured the
moment better than anyone, I believe, calling them
home on the radio in great style. Red Rum finished on
the stand side with Peter telling the listeners that Crisp
was out on his feet, and that Red Rum was going to
snatch the National – 'Red Rum, first, Crisp second, we
will never see a better finish in the National.' A great
climax. At Aintree and around the country, both Peter
Bromley and Peter O'Sullevan have had the use of
binoculars that were apparently rescued from German
U-Boats during the war, but serve a better purpose
today.

Before I made the switch to television, I covered
eight Grand Nationals for radio with Michael O'Hehir.
He was best known for calling the pile-up that
occurred in 1967, the year Foinavon won at 100–1. The
horse was miles off the pace at the time of the pile-up
but loose horses brought down all the runners in front
of him and he was able to jump the fence, which is now
named after him, at his leisure, and coast to victory.
That day Michael had the horses falling before they
had even hit the ground which was amazing. He used
to call me Mr Thomp-son which always made me
laugh. On National day, he would hitch a lift with a
police car across the course to the far side where the
commentary posts were – he might have been mis-
taken for a CID inspector in his old white macintosh.
As we passed through the crowds he would wave to
all the racegoers, shouting 'Enjoy yourselves!' He was
very popular and it's great that his son, Tony, is carrying on the family tradition for Irish television as well

as covering the Irish scene for the *Racing Post* so professionally.

Working at any National is a dream. Today, even after nearly two decades, I still miss it. It was my ambition to cover the race from the day in 1963 when I first enjoyed the National experience as a racegoer. I remember walking the track and wondering how on earth any horse could jump something as big as those fences. In those days, I used to stand behind the commentary box where Michael O'Hehir viewed the race, all good preparation for the day in 1973 when Michael told BBC Radio 2 listeners that he was about to hand over the commentary to me as the field progressed down the course.

After he won the race for the first time Red Rum became the centre of our radio broadcasts, yet when he beat Crisp, he was seen as a bit of a villain for stealing the race on the run-in after the famous Aintree Elbow about two hundred yards from the winning post. Crisp had been so brave, and nasty Red Rum had spoilt it all. But Rummy was soon converted into an Aintree hero, a racing hero and eventually a sporting hero – even a national hero, if you like. His own story made him a perfect focus for the Grand National day's radio broadcast. As everyone knows, his trainer, Ginger McCain, ran a second-hand car dealership at Southport and used to train Rummy on the beach. Every year that Red Rum ran we would go up to the stables in the morning and have breakfast with the McCains, and Brian Fletcher. Red Rum's owner, Noel Le Mare, said that he watched Rummy win his first National standing as 'still as a sphinx', while everyone around him was jumping up and down. He said afterwards that he was thinking how incredible it was that his horse was winning the world's greatest steeplechase.

I first set eyes on Rummy when my father had a runner at Wetherby where he was also due to make an
appearance. In those days he wasn't trained by the
McCains. His stable lass then said that Rummy was
only moderate, but the move to Ginger's yard trans-
formed him: he had bad feet and needed the soothing
effect of the salty water to stop him going lame.

Of the jockeys that were involved in the Red Rum
years Richard Pitman was a real star. After he had
been beaten on Crisp he did interviews where he must
have felt gutted, but he brushed off the disappointment by saying that he had enjoyed the greatest thrill
of his life in being so far in front on such a brave
jumper. I think he even went to Ginger's house for the
celebration party. Brian Fletcher was good value, too,
but in the end he lost the ride on Red Rum to Tommy
Stack, who eventually partnered the horse to his third
National win in 1977 after two second places. Brian, I
fear, will take a grudge to the grave about it, even
though he won three Nationals himself, two on
Rummy and one on Red Alligator in 1968 for Denys
Smith. Ginger felt that Brian's riding had cost Rummy
a victory in one of his preparatory races for the
National and decided to replace him but Brian still
argues that he was only saving the horse for the one
that mattered. In fact, Brian reckoned that Rummy
would have won four Nationals if Tommy had kicked
on earlier in 1976 as he felt the horse had a high cruis-
ing speed but not much turn of foot for a tight finish.

National day for me is a day by the television now,
watching one of the year's best racing broadcasts.
There is a *Morning Line* programme from London and
we have someone at the course to give an up-to-the-
minute report on the state of the ground and information about any runners who have been scratched
overnight. After that, I like to get home quickly and

settle down for *Grandstand*'s excellent programme. I'm always on the look out for new ideas and watching National *Grandstand* is a bit of homework. If there is anything I think we might use or adapt, I talk to Andrew Franklin about it when I next see him.

The BBC also covers the Welsh National from Chepstow – Channel 4 has to be satisfied with the Scottish National. 'Satisfied' is the wrong word: the Scottish National is one of the best races of the month and of the National Hunt season. Jumping at Ayr is great fun and has a special place in my heart: I presented my first steeplechase on television from there. There have been many memorable Scottish Nationals involving some of Scotland's best-known jumping figures – the Scots love a home winner – but I think the most emotional occasion was when Moorcroft Boy won the race in 1996. The horse had broken its neck falling at Aintree and it was a miracle that he survived, let alone was restored to a fitness level that enabled him to run in and win such a prestigious race. I have never seen his trainer David Nicholson so overcome with emotion as he was that day in the winner's enclosure. It was a moving occasion for everyone involved with the horse, as well as the Channel 4 team and Ayr racegoers.

The Channel 4 team would, of course, love to cover the Grand National, but at this time of year, we have already started to turn our attentions to the flat. By the start of April, Newmarket is beginning to buzz and the gallops are busy with trainers. The month is split by the Craven Meeting, with its Classic trials, which is the focus of both their attention and ours. My Newmarket home gives me an excellent vantage point to observe which trainers have their horses the most forward. David Loder's string is often the first to show its strengths up the Warren Hill all-weather gallop, and the big names – the Stoutes, Cumanis and Gosdens – begin to show their colours to the outside world after the weeks of indoor preparation. Paul Kelleway, a great jumps jockey and now a successful trainer, jokes that the gallops at this time of year can intimidate some of the smaller stables. The bigger strings make their appearance with a selection of well-bred stars, representing the best of two hundred or so horses back at the yard. In the morning, it can feel like Custer's last stand, Kelleway complains mischievously.

Around this time the difficulty for trainers with horses who are fancied for the next month's 1000 and 2000 Guineas is that you cannot rush them, and therefore April is a stressful month. Newmarket can be cold even then as it is flat and exposed. A horse can make its début at the Craven and then struggle to come on for a first seasonal run because of a drop in temperature. The trick is to get the horse to peak in time for the Guineas – but a few days of cold Suffolk wind can upset the best-laid plans, especially if the horse is a filly. It does not take much to put a filly heading for the 1000 Guineas behind schedule in April. They can even go downhill after running in the Craven Meeting's Nell Gwyn Stakes trial for the 1000 Guineas.

Away from the racecourse actions, the gallop watchers have to interpret what is going on, which stable's runners are coming to hand, and whose string will be spot on for the Guineas. This is a real gift. Watching a twenty-five-runner sprint on the racecourse, with all the horses identifiable from their coloured silks, is one thing, but following hundreds of galloping horses through binoculars and knowing who's who is another altogether. A host of people used to get up at the crack of dawn to study the horses working – a decade ago I can remember at least ten pairs of binoculars focusing on the new generation of three-year-olds at this time. Today, though, there are only three or four main operators: Tony Elves, who works for the *Sporting Life*, Tom Goff, of the *Racing Post*, David Milnes, who has an outstanding eye for a horse, and Geoffrey Faber, Goff's predecessor at the *Post*. Simon Crisford used to be a regular on the gallops, and Sheikh Mohammed makes several appearances with him throughout the year. One day I bumped into the boss when I was wearing a Newmarket sweat shirt and a Dubai jacket. 'Very international,' he remarked.

When I'm watching the gallops I like to interpret things for myself or talk over what I have seen with some of the town's head lads, who really know what's going on. Over the years some have become pretty good mates. I let them watch races on my television monitor during a racecourse broadcast and we swap information off air to good effect. Sometimes, though, you don't need confirmation of what you see: a good horse stands out. The 1996 1000 Guineas winner Bosra Sham impressed me on the gallops, even though as a three-year-old she had trouble with her feet. Before she won the Champion Stakes at the end of her Classic season, I saw her white face breeze past on the Newmarket Heath and leave her galloping companions almost standing. It was clear that she was in great form. Her trainer Henry Cecil came over to see what we had made of it and reckoned he hadn't seen anything like it since Wollow, a Classic winner for him in the 2000 Guineas at Newmarket in 1976. It was truly breathtaking. Sometimes you doubt what you've seen when they work as well as Bosra Sham did that day, but I backed her to win the Champion Stakes and on the racecourse she confirmed the impression she had given me. With her troublesome feet, they reckon she won the Guineas on three legs, but I wouldn't be surprised if she was good enough to win it on two. One of the greats, both on the racecourse and on the gallops.

Confirming that a horse has real ability before it runs – or identifying a horse who is running into form – is all about putting together all the different information you gather and all the whispers you hear. You have to interpret what you see, and think about who is giving you a tip and not just the tip itself. If Henry Cecil is thrilled with a gallop, as he was after Bosra Sham's work, then it's obviously worth taking note. It made sense to me to pay attention to the team training for Khalifa Bin Dasmal. Over the winter of 1995, he said to me that he thought he might win the Derby the following June with Shaamit. When I was back in Newmarket, William Haggas, the trainer, asked me over to have a look at the horse. He is married to Maureen Piggot, Lester's daughter, and his father-in-law was, like Shaamit's owner, convinced that the horse should take his chance at Epsom, even though he would be making his seasonal début. To me, Shaamit looked great, and he came highly recommended – by the greatest jockey of them all with nine Derbys to his name – so I backed him at 33–1. A nice winner that, come June. And it produced another. When I went to see the Haggas string, William was keen on a horse trained by Sir Mark Prescott. If you know that William was assistant trainer to Sir Mark before taking his own licence, you will understand that any such a recommendation should be noted. The horse in question was Pivotal who, during 1996, needed no further introduction. He won at Royal Ascot and at York. Again, it was the source of the tip that mattered – it is who is saying what that counts.

One of the most important aspects of the Channel 4 work I do is persuading people to talk for television and for the benefit of the viewers at home. Tony Elves has been on a few times and his views make good TV.

Some trainers do not like to see their travelling head lad in an interview before a big race, or the stable lad who looks after the favourite in the programme's feature race. I think they're worried that if the horse is reported to be working well and is then beaten, the stable may look unprofessional. Paul Kelleway has no fear of this and is a dream to work with. He had a fancied horse – Glory of Dancer – in Shaamit's Derby but still came on the Derby Day *Morning Line* and was open about the horse's chances. It gave the programme a real boost. Many trainers are superstitious about their horses being filmed before a big race. For whatever reason Luca Cumani is not especially helpful, and Michael Stoute is great for interviews but doesn't like his horses being filmed on the gallops. I think he may have had a bad experience in the past, or is worried that if something goes wrong – the horse drops the jockey or suffers an injury – it will be recorded for ever and repeated over and over again, which could be bad for business and his reputation. Before the 1000 Guineas, Henry Cecil did not want Bosra Sham filmed, but he had landed a big sponsorship deal with Saab and had to have an open day to announce it so we got the mare on film anyway. I don't think Henry was thrilled about it, but I'm sure that, in the end, Saab's money and Bosra Sham's 1000 Guineas win made him more than happy.

We on Channel 4 are not trying to be intrusive: racing needs television, as television means extra sponsorship, which means extra prize money, which is something I think everyone accepts that British racing needs. The better the programme, the better the viewing figures and the higher the sponsorship deals. I have received my fair share of criticism for interviews that some viewers have considered intrusive: I spoke to an emotional Henry Cecil after Bosra Sham had won the Champion Stakes and asked him if there had been some tears, and the following week's *Sporting Life* ran a few letters claiming that this was insensitive. I don't think it was: Henry is a complex, gentle man. I remember speaking to him as he drove out of the car park at Ascot just after the news became public that Sheikh Mohammed was moving forty horses from his stables. You could see the sadness in Henry's face at the end of such a long and happy partnership with an owner. But he is also a hard businessman, who knows the benefits to racing of television coverage. After all, before Bosra Sham ran in the Champion Stakes I asked him if he thought she would win and he turned the tables on me by asking what I thought! I think Henry is more than capable of looking after himself.

In racing we all have to remember that we are in the entertainment business, and that includes the jockeys. Look at Frankie Dettori. Today, he is brilliant on television. But not everyone in the weighing room is as helpful. Willie Carson used to come across as the chirpy Scot, but I never enjoyed a rapport with him. Naturally, along with everyone else, I always admired his riding immensely, but I thought that while he was still a jockey he had more to offer television and, indeed, he has ended up working for the BBC. Pat Eddery can sometimes disappoint a little, too. He doesn't give naturally and has his own way of going about things. But Pat will do his best for Channel 4 and you can't complain about his riding.

American jockeys are a revelation. The way they handle interviews straight after a race is great. I remember asking for an interview with Cash Asmussen just before a big race in Paris and, even though it was time for the horses to leave the paddock, he was happy to oblige. 'They'll wait for me,' he said. To be fair to European jockeys, Cash wasn't always helpful to the media. In the eighties I acted as his agent for a while. You'll remember that in 1988 he was disqualified from first place in the Ascot Gold Cup on Royal Gait. He lost his appeal against the decision and left the Jockey Club without comment so that we could sell an exclusive story to a newspaper.

Channel 4's cameras have done their bit for racing so it's not just a one-way relationship. The finish to the Whitbread Gold Cup at Sandown in 1991 was one of the race's most controversial. Cahervillahow, from Ireland, was first past the post, but was placed behind the runner-up, Docklands Express, after a stewards' inquiry. Cahervillahow's connections appealed against the Sandown stewards' decision as it looked as though the horse had won the race on merit. But Channel 4 footage from a camera positioned at a fresh angle showed that Docklands Express had suffered interference in the race and probably deserved to be placed first. The Channel 4 footage was decisive. I'd love it if we could have shown the stewards' inquiry – in fact, all inquiries – but apparently there are legal reasons why we cannot. The Jockey Club's Director of Regulations, Malcolm Wallace – I call him Big Mal, after the great football manager Malcolm Allison – has improved communications greatly between Channel 4 and the stewards, but hasn't been able to overcome the obstacles in the way of bringing the drama of the stewards' room to our viewers. I hope one day we can.

Until then, there is a sport to promote, and Sandown's Whitbread Gold Cup day, at the end of April, is a shop window for racing. It is the one meeting of the year that has absolutely everything – it doesn't need any controversy to make it more appealing. There is a great jumps race, after which the day is named, and top-quality flat racing, all staged at one of Britain's most popular racecourses. Whitbread Day is a great chance for the sport to sell itself generally, and the next few months' racing specifically, to the public. There is the first recognized Epsom Derby trial on the card so already we on Channel 4 are beginning to turn our thoughts and attentions to the world's most famous flat race. When racing and Channel 4 combine well for a great day's entertainment, the result is great television. Everyone benefits from that.

MAY

Classic Days

Months of anticipation come to a head in May for everyone who has a deep interest in flat racing. It is the beginning of the Classic season. Newmarket's second meeting of the year features D-Day for all trainers who have held out hopes over the winter of winning the 1000 Guineas, or the 2000 Guineas, the first of British racing's five Classic races. The expectations of winter will have risen or fallen with the Guineas trials of April but in May, over the Rowley Mile course, it's the real thing. Like the weather, things start hotting up for the colts in the 2000 Guineas and the fillies in the 1000 Guineas. Just eight more furlongs and the wait to know the year's Guineas winner is over.

The Guineas Ball, which was held for the first time in 1997 during the week before both races, got things going – until then, Newmarket had seemed a bit sleepy. Julie, along with Susie McKeever, Sarah Hedley and Michelle Fox, the former jockey Richard's wife, had organized it. It was a charity affair to raise money towards buying a fast-response vehicle to ferry doctors to the gallops, saving precious seconds when there has been an accident. Over five hundred people came for an evening with a Monte Carlo, Riviera, theme. John Reid and his wife, Joy, were voted the night's most glamorous couple, and another jockey, Gary Hind, won a Saab 2000 in the raffle – not bad for a fiver. In the charity auction, which I hosted, the best item – a VIP week's holiday at the Jebel Ali Hotel in Dubai – went to Jim Furlong, the racehorse owner, for his winning bid of £11,500. But Bernard Gover, the boss of Madagans, which used to sponsor the Guineas, matched the amount even though he lost out in the bidding. With generosity like that, it is easy to see how the evening raised over £50,000, which was £20,000 more than Julie and her team needed for the vehicle on which they had set their hearts. The extra went on some new equipment for the existing Newmarket ambulance and will help to cover the cost of sending ambulance staff on special training courses. A great night for everyone, which set things up perfectly for the following weekend's double header of Classics on the Saturday and Sunday. Let's hope it becomes an annual event.

The 1000 Guineas used to take place on a Thursday with the 2000 Guineas on the Saturday. The introduction of Sunday racing changed all that, and the two races now make up a great weekend of sport at Newmarket, the headquarters of British racing. Madagans helped enormously in developing the idea of a Classic racing weekend by offering group discounts and travel concessions, and should take a lot of the praise for any future success the concept enjoys. Credit where credit is due – especially as Madagans' business is debt-collecting.

That said, I'm not a huge fan of Sunday racing. It's great for racegoers, who no longer have to take a day off work to see both Classics, and I'm always happy to see more racegoers at the racecourse. But Sunday used to be a break from work for me. Nevertheless, I fully understand the logic behind Sunday racing and the benefits to everyone of a wider audience. Today, sport has to be run for the convenience of the spectators, and I'm glad they moved the Epsom Derby to Saturday from Wednesday. Some people said that the move would mean that the big corporations, which like to entertain at the races, wouldn't be interested in inviting guests to a Saturday Derby as it would cut into their clients' and partners' leisure time. Please! If you don't want to come to the Derby on a Saturday, you probably don't deserve to come on any day of the week. I've been to every Derby since 1971 and I used to have to leave early in the morning to make it to the track. These days, you can leave Newmarket at twelve thirty and be at Epsom by two.

Whatever the race day, Saturday, Sunday or midweek, my routine for a Newmarket meeting and an afternoon broadcast is the same, but the Guineas gives my work a special edge. Straight after *The Morning Line*, which always finishes at ten, a programme meeting is chaired by Andrew Franklin and this is when we decide on a running order for the afternoon's broadcast, and what items we will include in the programme. We're always exchanging ideas, especially Brough and I. Then the research starts, GG does his colours, Franks, John Oaksey, Alastair and Jimbo will be going through the form, and I dictate the afternoon's links between myself, Brough and the team. Even though it's close to home, there's no chance to nip back to the flat for lunch or a lie-down. Instead it's just a sandwich and maybe a coffee before I'm miked up for the afternoon and two hours of television and interviews. I have voices in my earpiece throughout the afternoon and keep a *Sporting Life* to hand with some notes to jog my memory. Hopefully, it's not rain-

ing as if it is I get pretty soaked outside all day! Whatever the weather, the programme is very demanding
and I have to admit that occasionally – just occasionally – I have written down one thing to say and come
out with the exact opposite. Just occasionally!

The Guineas unearths some of the best horses of
each year's generation. Nashwan's win in 1989 was a
truly great performance: he was making his seasonal
début and won for Major Dick Hern, the trainer. The
Major, as everyone calls him, is one of the old school
and is due to retire at the end of the 1997 season after
forty years of training. Brough had a big bet on
Nashwan to win the Guineas and the Derby and got
very excited after he won at Newmarket. Three weeks
before the Guineas, he had also heard about the gallop
Nashwan had completed at Major Hern's old West
Ilsley stable, which people said has been better than
anything even Brigadier Gerard, one of the best milers
of all time, had managed in 1971 and 1972.

Rodrigo De Triano's Guineas win in 1992 produced
one of the great Newmarket receptions in the winner's
enclosure. It was another Classic win for Lester Piggot,
back from retirement, and Newmarket, which can be
quite a reserved racecourse, cheered the maestro all
the way back to the weighing room. Rodrigo had been
beaten in the Greenham Stakes, his Guineas preparation race at Newbury, but Peter Chapple-Hyam never
lost faith in the horse. I admire Peter: he seems a very
precise trainer, great at having a horse ready exactly
for the big day.

These days, the Guineas meeting is especially interesting because the Godolphin horses who have wintered in Dubai have returned to Newmarket. It's the
first chance punters have to assess how big an impact
the warmth of the desert has had on the hand-picked
quality animals shipped east. In the Guineas, the effect

can be decisive. Mark of Esteem definitely benefited from a few months in the warmth. He showed that when he just edged out Bijou D'Inde, trained by Mark Johnston, and Mark Tompkins' Even Top in a three-way finish in 1996. Mark of Esteem proved again what a good horse he was later in the year in the Queen Elizabeth II Stakes at Ascot.

His Guineas win was controversial, though, as well as exciting. At Newmarket, they like to keep the horses on the track before the result of a photo finish is announced so that the winner can be given a proper reception by the crowd round the winner's enclosure. People applaud less if they don't know the result when the horses are led in. In Mark of Esteem's year, it was tense after such a close-run race. I went out on the track to be with the horses before the result was announced. When it finally came across the public address system that Mark of Esteem had won by the narrowest of margins, Frankie Dettori, who had ridden him, leapt clean out of the saddle with joy and hugged the horse's lad. He was so happy. However, in doing this Frankie had technically broken the rules: jockeys are not supposed to touch anyone before they have weighed in and Mark Tompkins, whose Even Top was confirmed as the runner-up, contemplated lodging an objection to the result. But it would have been outrageous if Frankie had been disqualified for jumping out of the saddle. I can see Mark's point of view, though. He explained to me afterwards that for him training is a business and he must explore for his owners every possibility to give them a winner. But, as I have already said, racing today is also entertainment and all Frankie was doing was expressing his delight and sharing his victory with the crowd who had remained in the grandstand to applaud the horses. He still had enough excitement left to repeat his trademark flying leap from the saddle in the winner's enclosure. Racing needs showmen like that.

Mark Tompkins is excellent with television cameras and always happy for us to film in the yard before a big race. Some trainers understand that racing has to be able to compete for spectators with other sports and Mark is one of them. Martin Pipe is another. I once organized a Duel of the Champions match at Warwick between Lester and John Francome, when both men were still riding, and Martin was more than happy to supply two evenly matched horses for the event. It was a one-off and it worked really well. It made *News at Ten*, so the sponsors were delighted. Martin also helped by persuading one of his owners to lend us a helicopter: Lester was riding at the Curragh in the afternoon and would have had a struggle to get back to Britain by six forty-five, the Warwick start time. He made it, but only thanks to Martin.

Trainers can let you down too, though. I suffered a major disappointment when I hosted a press conference a few years ago to announce the sponsorship of the trainers' championship by Pleasurama Casinos. I had arranged the sponsorship and invited plenty of trainers to support the event and give their views on the initiative so that the news would have a greater impact. Only four turned up and the sponsors withdrew after just one year, which was a big disappointment. Everyone who makes a living out of racing should help to promote the sport to as wide an audience as possible, jockeys and trainers, especially.

The lucky thing for racing is that the calendar promotes itself. Or, at least, it should. May is the month for the majority of Derby trials and, beginning with the Classic Trial on Whitbread Day at Sandown, they remind everyone to look forward to next month's big race of the year, and the rest of the season. Take the

Guineas. After the race, everyone starts talking about Epsom. Will the Guineas winner, who has shown his excellence over a mile, have the stamina for the extra half-mile of the Derby's twelve-furlong trip? Will connections decide to miss Epsom for Royal Ascot and confirm their colt as a potential champion miler instead? Could one of the fast finishers at Newmarket be more effective over the extended distance and reverse the placings at Epsom against the Guineas winner if he takes his chance? Or maybe the 1000 Guineas has thrown up the rare possibility of a filly running in the Epsom Derby instead of in the fillies' equivalent the Oaks? The countdown to the world's greatest flat race is well and truly on. Channel 4 shows all five Classics – the two Guineas, the Derby, the Oaks and the St Leger – and we need no invitation to start the clock ticking. Twenty days to Epsom, nineteen days to Epsom . . .

The Guineas itself, although a Classic in its own right, serves as a Derby trial and often gives the greatest insight into the race ahead of the actual event. It is, after all, Classic form that qualifies you for the rigours of Epsom and you cannot ignore good performances at the highest level. Nashwan didn't run between winning the Guineas and then the Derby. There was plenty of speculation about his pedigree and whether he would stay out the whole trip, which you must do to win at Epsom, and if he would handle the undulations of the switchback course. But what everyone knew after his Guineas win was that Nashwan had the Classic class to win the Derby.

Chester is quite like Epsom, a venue at which a horse has to be able to handle the track's tight bends and undulations. The three-day meeting in May is perfectly placed to host trials with the Derby meeting in mind and to test a horse's capacity to handle unusual configurations before it attempts to cope with Epsom's unique terrain. The Chester Vase, Chester Oaks and Dee Stakes are also chances for owners and trainers to test the stamina of their Derby and Oaks horses. In other words, they get answers to the two crucial questions: will the horse stay the Derby and Oaks trip of a mile and a half, and will it handle the Epsom switchback? To some extent the weather dictates the value of the Chester trials. If it rains, as it did in 1997 when racing was nearly abandoned and it felt like sub-zero temperatures by the paddock – the trials and their form can be worthless, unless the ground is similarly soft at Epsom. You have to judge for yourself.

The BBC used to cover Chester but gave up the May trials meeting. I was surprised and pleased. At this time, with less than a month to go before Epsom, Channel 4 is beginning to push the Derby and there's plenty of chat to be considered. Having three extra days' racing to broadcast now means that we can devote more programmes to the gossip already in circulation, and record and report events as they unfold – the action as it happens. It's busy. After racing, there's time for a plate of sandwiches and a frame of snooker with Franks at the Crabwall Manor Hotel, just outside Chester, where we stay – Franks is useless at snooker but he thinks he's a world champion in the making!

One year we tried to give viewers a real insight into how tricky Chester can be for horse and rider so that they might appreciate better the significance of a good run there to Epsom. The plan was to fit a camera in Franks's riding hat and then for him to ride round the course filming. Franks borrowed a horse, cantered him round gently, providing commentary to explain gently what the rider would be feeling at the different parts of the course with its twists and turns. The camera didn't work, so he did it again, this time on Gaasid, who was trained by Reg Akehurst and running in the Chester Cup. The finished item was good television, but there was quite a row next day when Reg's horse, who was quite fancied, finished fifth. The funny thing was that the horse Franks rode when the camera failed won at the meeting, so it can hardly have been the worst race preparation in the world. Since then, the Americans have developed a tiny camera, about the length of a lipstick container, which can be mounted on the right side of a jockey's helmet and linked to a transmitter the size of a cigarette lighter in his pocket.

York's Dante meeting provides perhaps the most informative test of the recognized Derby trials, and Channel 4 moves on there after Chester. I look forward to this meeting more than any other in the early part of the season, apart from the Guineas. It is a great track, flat and fair, and the ground is usually good. Everyone is so pleased to see you, at the racecourse, at hotels, in the city itself, everywhere. York is such a friendly place. Wherever you stay you're guaranteed a warm reception. I usually stay at the Mount Royal, run by the Oxenbys, which is packed with racing people. The season is in full swing and there's plenty to talk about. It's as if everyone has just come out of six months' hibernation.

John Smith, the clerk of the course, deserves a lot of the credit for turning York into the excellent venue that it is today. He used to work for Raleigh, the bicycle manufacturers, but has always been a respected horse-man among racing people on the northern circuit. One night I was having dinner with him and mentioned that the job was going at York and that he should apply. He didn't think he was experienced enough or sufficiently knowledgeable! Well, he's certainly proved himself wrong. John has ridden out at nearby Malton many times and understands the game, which is one of the reasons why he makes such a good clerk and why York is such a popular venue with trainers, owners, jockeys and, of course, racegoers. Get rid of the smell from the Terry's chocolate factory nearby and it would be perfect!

It is easier for a horse to look good and reveal its true potential at York than at Chester. It's a big, wide-open galloping track, and the best horse usually wins. True superiority can be disguised at Chester by the track's twists and turns. In the Chester Vase, Shergar looked impressive, but nothing like as dominant as when he won the Derby. The Dante meeting's big trial for the Derby is the Dante Stakes. If Shergar had run in the 1981 Dante Stakes instead of at Chester, he would surely have been able to stride out to reveal exactly how much better than the rest of the three-year-old colts he was that year. But York can fool you as easily as Chester, and provide a misleading impression to racegoers and viewers searching for clues. In 1993 I remember Tenby won the Dante in really impressive style, while in the Glasgow Stakes, a much less significant trial, Commander in Chief just narrowly edged in front on the line against a small, unimpressive, inexperienced field. In the end, though, when they faced each other directly at Epsom it was Commander in Chief who proved the best. Poor Pat Eddery. As both horses were owned by Prince Khalid Abdullah, who employed him as his retained jockey at the time, he had the pick, chose the wrong one and missed out on a Derby winner.

If a champion jockey can get it wrong, we can too. All the trials are a matter of interpretation. Take Slip Anchor. In the Lingfield Derby Trial of 1985, which along with Goodwood's Predominate Stakes completes the Derby trial season in England, Slip Anchor won easily but everyone said he didn't beat very much in the race. A week before the Derby, I listened to *Wogan*, the old television chat show, and Steve Cauthen, Slip Anchor's partner, was being interviewed. He said that Slip Anchor could have beaten any horse that day at Lingfield and that he would win the Derby. That was good enough for me!

It reminds me of Shaamit again. We filmed Shaamit and Glory of Dancer together on the Newmarket Heath in a gallop a short while before the Derby. Shaamit, who had not run that season, went right past Glory of Dancer, who was then Derby favourite. I decided I had just seen the horse I had expected to win the Derby turned over, so I backed Shaamit. William Haggas, who trained him, showed how skilled he is by sending the horse to Epsom to win on his seasonal début. Even the Stoutes, Cecils and Gosdens haven't managed that, although Saeed Bin Suroor did the same the year before with Lammtarra, who wintered in Dubai.

I think the thing to remember about all the trials and gallops at this time is that these are young horses who are developing and cannot be rushed. A lot can change in a short time. If the aim is to win the Derby, it is what they achieve in June that matters, not whether they win a trial. Lammtarra is a classic example. Three months before the big day in June, he was a sick horse. At the beginning of April when Julie and I left for Dubai at the end of the season, he still wasn't a hundred per cent. Even a week before the race, Sheikh Mohammed was still wondering if it was possible for a horse, who had suffered so recently from an abscess in his lungs, to win the Derby. The answer is yes, if they're as good as Lammtarra and patiently handled. Lammtarra hadn't even run in a trial before the Derby. A good trialist does not always win the Derby.

Lammtarra was fresh on Derby Day and it made the difference. By this stage in the season, keeping myself fresh is sometimes harder than working out the strengths and merits of horses galloping together on the Newmarket Heath. The evening racing season has begun and my commentating contract means I have to put in a few late ones for racegoers. With the heavy Channel 4 schedule, evening meetings and Sunday racing, it's quite a load. There is also work on videos to complete. There isn't really a break in the calendar until the week between Epsom and Ascot.

I've got a driver, Julian Coates, who helps shoulder some of the burden. It means I can sleep or learn the day's racing colours on the way to the racecourse. It is quite an unusual partnership. One year recently I was coming back from Doncaster and got talking to Julian. He explained that his wife had died and he had sold his business, which left him with a lot of free time. He said he loved racing and would probably be going anyway, so why didn't he drive me? It was a solid argument and we've been together ever since. Previously I had never trusted anyone to drive me – Brough especially. He's terrible. Julian is very safe. I call him Michael Schumacher because he never takes any risks or goes over fifty-five miles an hour. The only disruption he causes is when he interrupts an interview I might be doing to fill his autograph book. Luckily he has stopped doing that live on air!

The time Julian saves me by driving gives me a chance to flick through the Form Book, assessing and reassessing the strengths of the Derby trials before the big day. Or I might mull over a morning on the heath. Of course, gallops can sometimes tell you nothing. I remember Clive Brittain inviting me to watch User Friendly's last piece of work on the heath before the St Leger, which she went on to win. The gallop took place at four thirty in the morning and I couldn't see a thing! Some things are impossible to interpret.

JUNE

Derby Mysteries

The beginning of June marks about the eleventh week of the flat-racing year, which kicked off at Doncaster in March. But, in many respects, the start of this month marks the half-way point of the modern season, which nowadays extends to over thirty weeks. It is because the Epsom Derby takes place now and brings a sense that we are at the season's midpoint. The Derby is the ultimate test for three-year-olds and normally reveals the new Classic generation's star. Afterwards, the second half of the season can start when the three-year-olds face the older horses, who are four, five, and even six. The Derby is also the year's peak, which adds to that half-way house feel. Ask any jockey or trainer, even those who have already won it, and they will say that the Derby is the race they all want to win, Frankie Dettori included. The Epsom June meeting includes the Oaks – the fillies' Classic – and the Coronation Cup for older horses, both races, like the Derby, over a mile and a half. But although these two events are well worth winning, they are not the Derby.

For me, the Derby has stronger personal memories

than any other race in the year, both on the flat and over the jumps – even the National. It all started when I was thirteen. Every June I think back to when I first tuned in to hear the race commentary on the radio at Guisborough Grammar School. In those days, the Derby used to be off at three thirty-five which meant that I had to ask to be excused at the end of the three-thirty lesson to hear the thrills from Epsom. I'd be back at my desk by three-forty and no one would be any the wiser.

Every Derby is special, but some of my fondest memories are from the sixties: I recall Relko's Derby in 1963 and Santa Claus's in 1964, and the great Sea Bird, one of the best of all time, the following year. Sir Ivor's in 1968 also sticks in the mind – the late thrust by Lester Piggot that overhauled Sandy Barclay on Connaught. I remember that one so vividly because they brought out a film, *The Year of Sir Ivor*; I had joined the Racegoers' Club, which was just getting off the ground, and the club screened the film for its members.

The Derby leaves these strong impressions because it is unique, a one-off. The Epsom switchback track, shaped like a horseshoe, and the twelve-furlong trip is one of the most testing combinations in racing and means that the best horse nearly always wins the race. When I was working at Chantilly, I rode around the French Derby course there – you are allowed to work your horses on the track for a short while before their Derby, the Prix du Jockey-Club – and I cannot imagine that riding around Epsom is anything like as straight-forward.

The Downs also has a great history and tradition. In the old days, the in-field was packed with the fun fair and bookmakers, offering odds to once-a-year race-goers. On the far side to the grandstand, the home straight rail was lined with open-top buses right up to

Tattenham Corner. There was a real party atmosphere.

In the eighties and early nineties the atmosphere seemed to decline, but in 1997 it was right back, Benny The Dip's Derby. Walking around the Downs before the race, you could feel that everyone there, from the richest racegoer dressed in morning coat to those in jeans and a T-shirt, had come along for a special day. I went down to the start, which is across the Downs from the grandstand and finish line, for the beginning of the race. The stalls handlers and lads who were looking after the runners said that they could not remember so many people down by the stalls before the Derby for a long time. What was most amazing was that the morning's weather gave anyone who was in two minds about going an easy excuse to back out, but they didn't: 72,000 turned up. Epsom's racecourse management put on a great party.

That is how the Derby should be for the thousands of racegoers who come and for the millions who watch at home. Epsom could make the day even more exciting by bringing back the Oaks and the Coronation Cup to the Saturday too. In 1997 they were run on the Friday of a two-day meeting. There were 20,000 or so at the Oaks for Reams of Verse's win but on the Downs that sort of turnout is lost. The British Horseracing Board could also consider cutting back on other fixtures scheduled around the country on Derby Day. I don't think it helps betting turnover if races all over the country distract the punters from the season's main event. Why not make it racing's big day of the year? It deserves to be.

I am all in favour of another novelty they introduced in 1997 to make the Derby the special occasion it should always be: there was a military band and a male-voice choir to lead the crowds in songs like 'Land of Hope and Glory'. At Churchill Downs, before the

Kentucky Derby, they sing 'My Old Kentucky Home', which is really moving. The crowd loved it in 1997 before Benny The Dip's thrilling photo finish with Silver Patriarch.

Benny The Dip's Derby was enjoyed by plenty of Newmarket folk, myself and Julie included, as well as the thousands of racegoers also at Epsom that day. Everyone was thrilled for the winning jockey, Willie Ryan. Willie is one of the most popular jockeys in Newmarket, who has taken his fair share of knocks but has always bounced back. Winning the Derby was just reward for a hard grafter. I thought it was particularly tough on Willie that his main boss, Henry Cecil, had three runners in the 1000 Guineas at the beginning of the year, but didn't put Willie up on any of them. Well, the Derby on Benny The Dip was more than sufficient compensation. Full marks to John Gosden, the winning trainer, for recognizing Willie's quality and recommending him for the ride to the winning owner, Landon Knight.

Willie is a great mate and was best man at my wedding to Julie so you can imagine how thrilled I was for him. He rides out every day in Newmarket and is a dedicated race riding professional. I had tipped – and backed! – Silver Patriarch to win the Derby, but I didn't mind that he was beaten in such a tight finish. In fact, it was so close that even Willie said he didn't know if he had won. The two girls on horseback who accompanied him back to the entrance to the winner's enclosure said that they thought he had, while the video operators in the Channel 4 van, who are normally spot on, were vague. All I was hearing in my earpiece was 'We think he's won'. Poor Willie. When Lesley Graham, doing another of her horseback interviews, asked him, before the result of the photograph was announced, how he was feeling he could only say that he didn't know until the result was confirmed. Willie admitted later that Pat Eddery, who rode Silver Patriarch, seemed to act as though his horse had finished second and, according to Willie, Pat doesn't get it wrong very often so that calmed his nerves. Then, it came over the tannoy, and Willie knew that he'd done it.

On the Saturday evening after the Derby, it was open house at the Ryans' with Willie's proud father, Denis, who had been a jockey himself, in attendance. We all wanted to watch a video of the race, but Willie didn't have one. He'd banned anyone from doing a tape as he thought it might bring him bad luck. I have a feeling that Denis wasn't too sure how to work the video camera anyway. After a while, we all left the Ryans' and moved on to the Plough in Ashley, which by ten-thirty that evening was bulging. Every jockey in Newmarket was there – they had applauded when Willie went back to the weighing room after the Derby. I wouldn't like to have seen the bar bill, but it was one of the great nights for the town. I hope that Willie starts getting more opportunities now that he has proved to everyone beyond any doubt that he's got what it takes.

My own professional high point at the Derby came with radio eighteen years before Willie's great moment. It was the two-hundredth Derby and Des Lynam was due to present a double-header of sport: racing from Epsom and a European Championship qualifier for England against Bulgaria from Sofia. I got a call on the morning of the Derby to say that Des wasn't well and that I would have to substitute for him. Well, you can imagine what this meant to me at the time – and still does. It was a brilliant Derby. Troy was fantastic and Willie Carson, who rode him, was in top form in interviews afterwards, as good as he had been in the saddle. I remember Peter Bromley's commentary: 'And here comes Troy from nowhere.' England won 3–0, which was also great. I was on a high and I ended the broadcast with what I still feel is one of the best sign-offs of my radio career: 'The crowds are leaving Epsom, some richer, some poorer, some a little worse for wear. But they were here for the two-hundredth Derby and saw one of the greatest Derby winners ever.' I received a lovely letter from Don Mosey, the 'Alderman' of Test Match Special fame, who said that he found it all very moving. I slept well that night.

Shergar is the other Derby winner lodged in my mind. I remember Shergar particularly because he was at the centre of one of the strangest weeks of my life. As everyone knows, Shergar, who carried the Aga Khan's famous silks to win at Epsom in 1981, was kidnapped from his owner's Irish stud and never seen again. The colt was outstanding at Epsom, ridden by Walter Swinburn. My own part in the Shergar mystery – no one knows what happened to him – came about when I was selected by a man claiming to be the kidnapper to negotiate the horse's return. I was working for ITV at the time. The way things developed was so amazing that I recorded my thoughts nine days after it all happened.

Audio Transcription / Thames TV
Thames Sport: *Shergar*

This is Derek Thompson with recollections of the Shergar story as it affected me.

I don't know how long the telephone had been ringing, but when I woke up I reached over and picked up the receiver. I thought it was a man telling me that it was now half-past seven, giving me my early-morning call. He mumbled a few words and I didn't really understand him, so I had to say: 'What time is it?' He said: 'It is the unearthly hour of a quarter to two in the morning.' It was at this point that I actually woke up and asked the man what on earth he was phoning me about. He said he was from the Press Association in London and was phoning to tell me that I had been named as one of the three journalists the kidnappers – the supposed kidnappers – of Shergar wanted to talk to. They apparently wanted John Oaksey of the [*Daily*] *Telegraph* and Peter Camplin of the *Sun*, and myself to fly to Belfast to stay at the Europa Forum Hotel, be there on the Thursday evening and to await instructions as to where to go to get Shergar back.

I asked him [the PA man] to repeat it all again, and eventually we got it all sorted out. After talking to him for about five minutes I then tried to get back to sleep but, of course, it was totally useless. I kept thinking about the horse. I kept thinking perhaps it wasn't the kidnappers who wanted me but some terrorist organization in Northern Ireland. The heart started pumping a bit and I don't think I slept too well after that. Then the phone calls started coming at about seven in the morning. The first one was from Bob Champion. Bob said: 'They want you over in Belfast to get the horse back, I've just heard it on breakfast television.'

When I arrived at the office, the press officer for Thames Television was putting out stories about me, how I present *Thames Sport*, giving my life story, sending out photos of me. He seemed to be enjoying it all. I talked it all over with Phil King, the editor of *Thames Sport*, and also Bob Burroughs, the executive producer who was in contact with Ron Allison, head of sport for Thames, who was in Geneva, and we talked about whether I should go to Belfast or not. I'd already at the time been in contact with John

Oaksey, and he said he was flying out on the shuttle but, of course, this was programme day for me. I had to present *Thames Sport*. But we all agreed that the best thing was to go to Belfast (a) to try and help get the horse back and (b) to do a piece, obviously, for *Thames Sport* on the latest situation.

The Europa Hotel is where all the journalists stay, so there were plenty of them already in the foyer, and as I was checking in, literally within seconds of arriving, there was a tannoy message – there is a call for Mr Derek Thompson. So I went over to the telephones in the foyer, picked it up and the man said: 'Mr Derek Thompson?' in a sort of a Southern Irish accent, perhaps just south of the border, quite cool, not cultured, but, um, normal-sounding voice. And he said to me: 'You are the one who does the ITV?' I said yes.

He said, 'What did you do before that?'

I said, 'Well, I was on Radio 2 for about nine years doing the sport on there.'

'Oh, oh,' he replied, at which point I thought it fair to ask who was calling. He said, 'My name is Arkle.'

I said, 'As in the horse?'

He said, 'Yes. We have got Shergar.' Then it struck me that here we were in Belfast and this was what it was all about. 'Now listen, this is what I want you to do,' he said. 'Get in touch with Mrs Jeremy Maxwell.'

I said, 'The Maxwells, she's the wife of the trainer?'

'Yes,' he said. 'Give them a ring at this particular number.' So I was told to ring, he gave me a number. 'And you'll then be given further instructions as to what to do.' And then the telephone went dead.

I made the phone call to the number I had been given. A man answered. I said: 'Is that Mr Jeremy

Maxwell?'

'No, they're out.'

I said, 'Well, this is Derek Thompson from ITV. I am one of the journalists who's been called over to negotiate the release of Shergar.'

He said, 'Ah, yes, I've heard about you. Well, they're not back at the moment, would you call back?'

I said, 'Well, I've been told to call this number, who am I talking to? Are you the head lad or a stable lad?'

He said, 'No, I'm a law man.'

I said, 'Well, listen, we – we've been told to come out there.'

He said, 'Well, ring back in five minutes and I'll tell you how to get here.' I rang him back in five minutes and he told me how to get there, thirty miles outside Belfast. And he also said that just before I got to this isolated farmhouse about a quarter of a mile away, two men would jump out in front of me. They would be armed men, but they would be policemen. I said, 'Oh, they'll be in uniform?'

He said, 'No, no, plain clothes. They will identify themselves and they will give directions to travel further. And although you won't see them, the house is [also] surrounded by police.' This was when it began to dawn on me that we were in Northern Ireland and anything could happen. If I could lose all the journalists from the hotel they [the police] would certainly appreciate it. I got the head of security for the hotel up to ask how to get out without the journalists knowing. So we [John, Peter and I] proceeded down in the lift, through the kitchen, out the back door, and got to the car which the security man had taken round to the back. We couldn't get the key in the lock. But, anyway, we managed eventually, jumped in the car, and roared off down the street, sometimes at ninety miles an hour.

Within an hour we were close to the Maxwell farm, only to be reminded how potentially dangerous our situation was. Just a few minutes away from Jeremy Maxwell's, five men in balaclavas with machine guns jumped out in front of the car, ordering us to stop. The car screeched to a halt. One of the men motioned to me to wind my window down and asked me if I was Derek Thompson. I didn't know whether to say yes or no. Luckily, as I had been warned, it was the police and they gave us the final directions but it still scared me to the bone.

When we arrived at Jeremy's, he came out and said, 'Don't park there, park round the back, quick.' So we parked round the back, rushed into the house, where we met Judy Maxwell, Jeremy's wife, and Richard Pitman who had been staying nearby, trying to buy some horses from Jeremy.

Apparently, the guy who called himself Arkle had rung Jeremy first, but it was a bad line, the phone went dead and when he rang again Jeremy was in the loo. Judy took the call and it was Judy to whom the man was talking after that. They had a call to go down to the hotel not far away, where they would be contacted again, but by the time they had got there, the man had just called and before they could get to the phone he had rung off. So they came back. They were waiting for another call so we all sat down and waited.

Before the three of us arrived there, Arkle had said that he was asking for a ransom of one thousand pounds a share[holder], and as there are forty shares in Shergar, that's forty thousand pounds, which is nowhere near the two million pounds which apparently was originally asked for. He said he wanted this made public, and he also stressed that the horse, although not in his usual surroundings, was being well cared for and was very comfortable. The caller also changed his code name from Arkle to another famous horse [Ekbalco], which I wasn't allowed to disclose.

It was about eight-thirty when Ekbalco called again. I talked to him and he repeated his request of forty thousand for the horse and stressed that he wanted that made public, broadcast on the BBC news. So he would then ring us back and give us further instructions. We talked a little while after that and wondered whether this was a hoax or not. The general opinion we got was that it was not a hoax, so I took it in my mind to ring the Aga Khan. I rang his Irish stud and talked to Ghislain Drion, the manager, and told him of the call we had had. He said, 'Listen, don't tell me, tell the man the Aga has sent over', presumably his right-hand man, to deal with the kidnapper. He gave me his name as David Watson, a well-spoken Englishman. I got the impression as I was telling him what had happened that he didn't really seem too interested and after talking for about five minutes I began to feel that he just wasn't interested at all in what we had to say. He thought everything we were doing was a hoax. So I stressed the point again about what had happened, and what the man now called Ekbalco wanted us to do and said, 'Would you please give the Aga a ring and get back to us one way or the other. Or you think about it and then give me a call back.' He said he'd call me back in the morning. I repeated that this could be too late. Couldn't we get a call through tonight to the Aga? He said he would do his best. We said goodbye. I was totally frustrated by this call. It was as if he thought I was a journalist ringing up for the latest news, rather than the go-between who was trying to get Shergar back. And we were the official – well, the unofficial, if you like – go-betweens at this stage. We had no reason to believe it was a hoax.

About half-past ten, we got a call from a woman who said she was phoning on behalf of the Aga. The Aga came on the line, Jeremy Maxwell talked to him and we recorded it. Now I've interviewed the Aga, and he has an exceptionally deep accent, deep voice. And this man sounded exactly the same as the Aga. He just asked how much was being asked and said he would ring back. Half an hour later, he did. And it was at this point that he said, 'Proceed, we'll pay.' We immediately rang the BBC and they put it out on their 11.45 p.m. news, before closedown, that the Aga had agreed to pay the ransom of £40,000. We had no reason to believe that this was a hoax call as I had phoned the stud two to three hours previously. So we thought the stud had rung the Aga who then phoned us. We only realized it was a hoax when we played back the interview six or seven times. At the end of one of his sentences, he said 'you know', which is not really a thing that the Aga would finish a sentence with. And that is why and when we decided it was a hoax call.

Ekbalco was back on the phone again. He said, 'Right, we want a goodwill gesture for a picture of the pony. I'll ring you back and let you know the instructions.' A few minutes later he rang back, they wanted a thousand pounds in fives and ones for a picture of the pony. He rang again and it was me talking to him. He said, 'Listen, we want this money for this photo.'

I said, 'Well, how do we know the photo will have

been taken recently? Could you put a morning paper next to the photo so at least we can get the date off the top and know that the horse is still alive?'

He said, 'This will happen,' and then rang off.

At ten past one he came through again. 'Derek, I'm beginning to think that you suspect that I'm a hoax.'

I said, 'Put yourself in my position. What would you think if a guy kept on ringing up all the time the way you do?'

And he said, 'Well, I am not a hoax. We have got Shergar and if you don't give us the money by nine a.m. we'll shoot him.'

We got a call from the BBC newsroom in Belfast. They said that they had had a call from a man called Arkle. Now not many people knew that this was his first code name. He was saying that he was getting fed up and getting no joy at all.

About half-past two in the morning I tried to get my head down upstairs. Tried to go to sleep. I don't think I slept more than five minutes. Shortly after 7 a.m. came the call we were all dreading. 'Hello, this is Arkle, the horse has had an accident and we've put him down.' It was at this point that the police said they now knew it was a hoax because the kidnappers wouldn't have destroyed the horse. I went back to the hotel at this stage. I felt a bit depressed, obviously.

The next day, I got a message saying: 'Trident in the sea, what comes out of the top of a bottle?' Which perhaps sounds very stupid, and doesn't even rhyme. But I had been told that the code name for the kidnappers, supposed kidnappers, calling the Aga's stud, was King Neptune. Trident in the sea? King Neptune? What comes out of the top of a bottle? A cork. King Neptune in Cork. We rang the police. They said they thought it was a hoax.

I was very tired when I got home on Saturday night – from Belfast, via Ayr, after presenting the racing on television – to Yorkshire. Since then I have slept all right, but I seem to wake up in the middle of the night thinking about Shergar and trying to work out actually what happened to him. Is he dead? Is he alive? Was it a hoax call? Was it a real call? Perhaps the police know more about it, perhaps secret negotiations are going on. I think the horse is dead. Let's hope not, perhaps they'll find him soon. At least I won't have it on my conscience for the rest of my life that the calls we had were real. Just think if I hadn't gone and the horse was [then] killed.

My efforts to secure a safe return of Shergar from the hands of kidnappers was a bizarre departure for me. I had never been involved in anything quite like it before and I do not expect to be involved in anything like it again.

Interviewing on the move has always been part and parcel of my work. This is very much the case at the Derby, when the build-up for the big race involves so many different people from all walks of life. You have to cover so much ground and also need to spread the atmosphere of the occasion through the whole programme. That means speaking to owners, trainers, jockeys, and the rich and famous from other sports and the world of entertainment who descend on the Downs. The Channel 4 Derby audience is not made up of the same viewers as a normal Saturday show from, say, Newmarket. The programme's content has to be more popular, so all the time we are on the lookout for unusual interviews. After the race has been run, things are a little more straightforward. Then it's a case of grabbing the winner. But even that can cause a few nervous moments. I remember asking Lester Piggot how he felt after he had won the Derby on Teenoso in 1983. He was still in the saddle, and, with camera flashes popping everywhere, all he would say, out the corner of his mouth, was 'Sod off.' It was lucky that the maestro's own peculiar way of talking and the distance he was from the microphone muffled his response and spared any embarrassment in front of a huge television audience. Something for Lesley Graham to be wary of next time she interviews a Classic winner on horseback.

Interviewing the winning connection of the Derby should be the easiest job in the world. If you have just won the Derby you are on a major high, and any interview should make great television. But people do get a bit emotional and that can mean they really struggle to express the excitement of having watched their horse win the world's greatest flat race. Shaamit's owner, Khalifa Bin Dasmal, was so nervous before the race that he rang me up to ask me if I thought he would win, so you can imagine how excited he was after the result. The Aga Khan was the exception: he's always very composed – but I suppose he must have got used to winning the Derby. He has enjoyed tremendous success in the race. I found it hard to tell how the owners of Secreto, who won the race in 1984, were feeling as they spoke only Spanish. All I could work out was that they owned a bus company in Venezuela! When I was interviewing Henry Cecil after Commander in Chief's Derby in 1993, the problem was altogether different. Then, I simply couldn't hear him as the brass band that is always positioned near the winning post struck up a rousing tune just as Henry was about to explain what it had been like to see his stable's other runner Tenby, the odds-on favourite,

A lifetime apart From the eight-year-old Stockton boy who tried his best to grab a bite from a washing-line of doughnuts, to the man who today seeks the views and opinions of horse-racing's stars, and gives worldwide audiences the benefit of more than twenty years' experience as a broadcaster at the heart of the sport.

Channel 4 through the years Since becoming part of the team in 1985, Derek has joined many a programme meeting with valued colleagues past and present (*above*, before racing at Sandown) in preparation for moments with turf celebrities (Desert Orchid, *below*) and interviews with jockeys (Graham Bradley, *top right*). *Right*: Sharing the mike with John Francome, and appearing with fellow team members John McCririck and Brough Scott.

Racing pro
In his years on radio and television at the centre of events, Derek has quizzed the influential figures of the Turf all over the world. Sheikh Mohammed (*opposite top*) is at the centre of racing in the Middle East; Walter Swinburn (*middle, at Epsom where in 1981 he partnered Shergar, who has featured large in Derek's life*) is one of the game's great achievers and Jack Berry (*bottom left*) one of its stalwarts; then there is the great Pat Eddery (*left*), and his fellow professionals' professional, John Reid, (*below*).

The common touch Derek's involvement in racing, from the trainer's stable to the commentary box, has seen him interview princesses (Anne, The Princess Royal, at Newmarket, *above*) and out-ride future kings (HRH The Prince of Wales, at Plumpton, *below*), as well as bring celebrities of sport and society into viewers' living rooms (*top right*, Lady Lloyd-Webber, *middle right*, boxer Chris Eubank and *bottom right*, football's Jack Charlton).

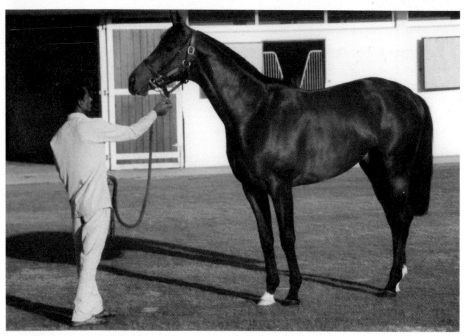

All play, no work Away from the pressures of broadcasting, Derek still enjoys racing company (Newmarket trainer Robert Williams hitches an aqua lift, *top*) and the pleasures of ownership (the Thompson-owned Lion Tower, stabled in Dubai, *above*). The occasional moment of unscheduled sleep if a Francome book fails to entertain (*below left*), and the more frequent off-screen cigar (*below right*), are relaxing and an important break from the microphone.

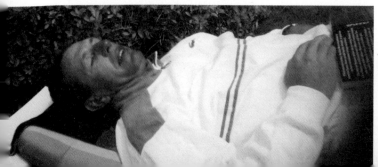

overhauled by the yard's less fancied second string.

Interviewing celebrities at the Derby is quite differ-ent from quizzing racing people. We have to talk to soap stars and anyone from the world of sport and general entertainment, which can be difficult as some-times I don't really know exactly what they're famous for. I'm not a telly-addict and need to be well briefed on *Emmerdale* and the like. The other problem is that, to some degree, it's the same celebrities every year. Joan Collins is a real superstar, the real McCoy, and Brough and I used to joke with each other about who would have the chance to interview her when it was con-firmed that she was coming to Epsom again. But after a few years, even with someone as famous as Ms Collins, it's oh, no, not Joan again. Having said that, chatting to the stars can be really great. A lot are really into their racing. I remember Steve Harley, the star of rock band Cockney Rebel, telling me about his affection for the Derby. He recalled a big bet that he had had on Shergar. He was performing in Germany during the afternoon of the race and could not be at Epsom, but he was not going to miss the action on television. He finished per-forming just in time and left the stage to find a tele-vision and never bothered to come back for an encore. The fans weren't too happy, but Steve was. He bought a new car out of his winnings, a top-of-the-range BMW.

One interview I definitely didn't carry out was with Lord Lucan. I was rung up by the *Sunday Sport* a few years ago to ask if they could quote me in one of their stories. Thinking it was no more than the paper up to a bit of mischief, I agreed. The *Sport* then printed a story headlined 'TV Presenter Sees Lord Lucan at Epsom' with the story underneath in which tele-vision's Tommo was reported as saying that it was cer-tainly him! They had superimposed Lucan's face on to a racegoer's.

It is great to meet all these famous people – if not Lord Lucan! – but on Derby Day I would prefer just to enjoy the atmosphere of the Downs and the camaraderie. It's one of my ambitions to travel by open-topped double-decker bus to the Derby and park alongside the home straight for all the excitement of the finish. Tommy Steele, the great entertainer, summed it up for me when I interviewed him one year. He recalled his father taking him on to the Downs aged five for the great atmosphere of those days and seeing five seconds of horses through people's legs as they raced round Tattenham Corner. That is what the Derby is all about. A day out. Not the Roger Moores, the George Hamiltons – or even Joan Collins.

Celebrity racegoers fit in much better at Royal Ascot. This will never be a punter's meeting: it's all about the glamour of the Turf and what is good about English racing. It's the sport's shop window and any extra glitter added by celebrities from television, film, music and sport helps to widen racing's audience for the future. For me, the four days of Royal Ascot used to be the busiest of the year when I was working full-time in radio. The Radio 2 programme would be broadcast from the track and presented by someone like Jan Leeming, Pete Murray or Gloria Hunniford. I would rush around interviewing people like Bing Crosby (and Linda Lovelace, of the film *Deep Throat*). It was the beginning of the wider-style racing coverage by radio that we all enjoy on Radio 5 Live today. Bing Crosby was an old man when I interviewed him, but he came alive when he was on air. Contributions like the one he provided gave the programme – and racing – appeal to a broader audience with added depth, too. Even though the racing at Ascot on all four days is second to none, we needed the celebrities to sustain the interest of a wider radio audience. The presenters were celebrities in their own right, too, which helped. Jan Leeming was a good sort and Pete Murray was a real old hand.

The Royal Meeting is the BBC's big racing fixture of the year so I am not working there for Channel 4 – or SIS, or the Racing Channel, for that matter, as I have never commentated at the Royal Meeting for racegoers. Instead, I have a heavy week of tipping, pre-racing personal appearances and speech-making, marking the cards of racegoers, hopefully with some winners. With the racing attracting plenty of Irish runners, I am on the phone to Sean Hehir, my contact in Ireland. Sean (no relation to Michael Hehir) is chairman of AIG, which sponsors the Champion Hurdles. He has a box at the Curragh – in 1996 he was invaded, in the nicest possible way, by the Niarchos family when they watched their own Spinning World win them the Irish 2000 Guineas – and is close to all the top racing people in Ireland.

The great thing about a week like this is that I can really enjoy the racing along with everyone else, once I have got the morning and lunchtime work out of the way. In the past, Julie and I have been guests of George Ward, who hosts a party every year, in the room next to the one booked by the Sangsters. It's a lovely occasion, one of the social highlights of the year for us, a real treat.

In the afternoon, before the day's big race, I like to go to the pre-parade ring at the top end of the course. It's a chance to have a close look at the best horses in training, which is a rare privilege. You meet all sorts at the pre-parade ring at Ascot. You can end up standing next to anyone – racegoers, punters, the Aga Khan, Princess Margaret . . . It's a great mix. One year, when I was standing near Princess Margaret she pointed towards me and said to one of her party, 'He knows what he's talking about, ask him.' Very flattering.

Ascot really is a tremendous four days of racing. If you spend the whole week there it's hard to imagine there's anything wrong with the sport. The pageantry of the Royal Family's procession before racing disguises some of British racing's problems, like low prize-money. Training fees in Britain are incredibly high and hard-headed businessmen like Peter Savill, who spend millions on racing, expect a better return on what they consider an investment. I don't know what the answer is. Fleecing the bookmakers isn't. They want to make a profit, and why shouldn't they? A Tote monopoly would help financially because all the Tote's profits stay in racing through race sponsorship and grants to racecourses. But a Tote monopoly, with only pool betting, is a non-starter, anyway: it may work in other countries, but it would kill a lot of the atmosphere at our racecourses. I know what racing without bookmakers is like from my time in Chantilly: boring. I think expanding the Tote could help: why not have terminals in newsagents next to the machines that print out lottery tickets?

Some trainers are better than others at making the best of things in Britain. Ben Hanbury is great at attracting owners to the sport and Conrad Allen, another Newmarket man, offers owners incentives and discounts if they pay training fees early. These are the sort of things you need to consider if an owner has a horse who struggles to win at Catterick, let alone land a big prize at Royal Ascot. But racing must also help itself before it starts looking elsewhere for handouts. We could look after sponsors better. Sometimes they are not given the thanks they deserve for supporting a race and even the smallest contribution should be fully acknowledged. If a sponsor thinks they are not getting value for money, the racecourse should ask why, so that they don't leave the sport to support something else instead. We should also be on the look-out for new sponsors and sponsorship opportunities. I think it is probably the time to allow sponsorship at Ascot, which would make a lot of money for the sport.

These problems are not on the menu for discussion after a week at Royal Ascot. When I have done four journeys from Newmarket to Berkshire and back for the full week's racing I'm pretty shattered. Certainly too tired to try to solve all the conundrums of British racing over the weekend. I look forward to the Saturday of Ascot Heath and a well-earned day off.

At least, I usually do. Except in 1996 I had something rather important to attend to. I got married to Julie! In fact, it was virtually the only weekend of the summer that Andrew Franklin was prepared to allow me – and the Channel 4 team, many of whom came as guests – to take a holiday. With Ascot the week before, I didn't have a stag night of legendary proportions. I'm not really up for that any more, to be honest. I remember too well the first such occasion I ever attended. It was during my Radio 2 days and after a night at the old Playboy Club I ended up sleeping over at 'Diddy' David Hamilton's house in Barnes. Ian Darke, the box-ing commentator who was also part of the sports desk, snoozed all night upside down on the stairs. That memory was enough to keep me on the straight and narrow when the stag night came up for me.

The wedding was on the Saturday morning at Ravenwood Hall, Roughman Green, just outside Bury St Edmunds. We had explored the possibility of a registry office but didn't like the idea and Ravenwood Hall was perfect. There were about twenty-five close friends, including Howard, my brother. Willie Ryan was officially my best man, but as he was riding at Redcar that day Howard did the honours at the service. Willie took over for the reception, at Newmarket racecourse. After some lunch, we had a break so that everyone, including me, could watch the European Championship quarter-final at Wembley between England and Spain. By the evening all our racing friends had returned. What a night. I hope it was worth the journey for everyone, many of whom had made such an effort to be there. The Off-Beats, a band fronted by Julie's brother Steven Summerfield, provided a mix of seventies music and disco hits. Richard Dunwoody and Michael Hills were the last to leave. William Haggas had to apologize to three different women the following day for one thing and another. It was a really special occasion and great to be surrounded by two hundred dear friends who were all able to let their hair down.

Our honeymoon was mind-blowing. We travelled 27,000 miles in total, saw Tom Jones in Las Vegas, visited Hawaii, and stayed at the Beverly Hills Hilton, where they filmed *Pretty Woman*, Julie's favourite film. It was unbelievable. It made me feel as important as one of the celebrities I'm used to interviewing at Epsom or Ascot. In fact, we tried to book a table at the Polo Lounge and were refused until someone from England told the manager that I was a television presenter. After that we were treated like stars!

Of course, admitting that you're on television isn't always the most sensible thing to do. When John Francome was pulled up for speeding a few years ago and tried the 'I'm in television and very busy' routine to get off a fine, he had picked a policewoman who knew nothing about racing and didn't care how many winners he had ridden! Bob Champion had a different experience. He was recognized, but he still got fined.

Champ must have thought he would get off after he was asked for his autograph, but the policeman just said, 'Thanks. Now exactly how fast do you think you were going?' It was certainly well over the speed limit. But that's jockeys for you. As Mick Ryan, the Newmarket trainer, always complains, they leave late to arrive early!

JULY

Sports of Kings

Why do people go away in July for their holidays? I just don't understand it. The middle of summer is such a great time for all sport, especially July. The Open Golf Championship, Wimbledon, and every four years the Olympics and football's World Cup. Why miss any of it? The only good reason I can come up with is if you have the chance to marry someone like Julie. Our honeymoon after the wedding in June clashed with the Wimbledon tennis, which was the only minor drawback to this happy event taking place in the middle of the usual busy summer of sport. Frankly, I wouldn't miss the sport in July for anything less important.

Most racing people are also fans of other sports. The competitive instincts of the racing fraternity are shared by their counterparts in other sporting disciplines.

Horseracing folk love the Open Golf Championship and many are enthusiastic players. Especially the jockeys. Richard Hills is a bit like his father, Barry, the trainer, on the course. Barry Hills' nickname is Mr Grumpy and Richard can become a bit moody if the putts aren't dropping. The odd club has followed a

Hills mis-hit drive into the rough or some water. John Carroll is the opposite: always a smile. Richard Hughes hits the ball a mile for a jockey. An unlikely golfing partnership is John Francome and Steve Smith-Eccles. 'Franks' jokes today that when he was riding he never imagined he would end up such a keen player, especially with the 'Eck' as a partner. He played at Chester a few years ago for the first time and couldn't even hit the ball, yet now he plays virtually every day during the summer. He has been well and truly bitten by the bug. Graham Goode, from the Channel 4 team, enjoys a game once a week. He even managed a round at Troon in Scotland where the Open has been played. The starter at Troon is a great racing fan: give him the year's winner of the Ayr Gold Cup and you'll find it a lot easier to secure a civilized tee-off time.

I love watching the Open. Players like Nick Faldo seem to soak up pressure. People who criticize golfers for 'bottling it', as some say Greg Norman did in the 1996 US Masters, are being unfair. It's nonsense. Just imagine what it must be like. I play off a handicap in the low twenties so I can't pretend to appreciate exactly what the stress feels like, but I can see with my own eyes what professional golfers have to go through. In some respects jockeys are lucky: if they ride a poorly judged race there's usually another straight away for them to get back in form and ride a winner. Golf isn't like that. I remember the television commentary by Henry Longhurst when Doug Sanders missed a putt of less than a yard on the seventy-second green, which would have won him the Open at St Andrews in 1970. It seemed that as soon as Sanders hit the putt, Longhurst knew, and said, 'He's missed it.' That putt plagued Sanders for the rest of his career. It meant he tied with Nicklaus and lost the Open in a play-off.

I've had my moments on the golf course. I played Ben Hanbury once on the nine-hole Worlington course near Newmarket for a tenner. Ben brought along his dog whom he claims can find the ball every time, but this proved no advantage to him. I virtually parred my way round and Ben packed it in after just nine holes when we'd planned to play a full eighteen. As he walked off I called to him about the tenner and he shouted back that he'd put it on a runner he had that afternoon. The horse bolted in at 3–1. My lucky day.

As well as its well-documented links with football and footballers, racing also enjoys a great relationship with cricket. There are not many Test matches and county-cricket dressing rooms without a well-thumbed copy of the *Racing Post* or the *Sporting Life*. Dennis Lillee, the legendary Australian fast bowler, is a keen punter, and some players have bought the odd leg in training. Michael Holding, the former West Indies fast bowler, has had the odd interest over the years and is a great friend of the Newmarket trainer Michael Stoute, who was born in Barbados. I've met both Michael Holding and Dennis Lillee. You would expect them to be formidable company, but Michael has the softest voice and gentlest handshake you could imagine, while Dennis is more interested in UK financial futures than boasting about his bowling average. I had lunch with Dennis and all he wanted to know was what I thought might be a good investment for him.

The two summer Olympic Games I have covered provided me with some of my greatest personal sporting memories. I commentated on the equestrian events at both Moscow and Seoul. My media accreditation for the games was 'D. Thompson' but I opted out of joining my competing namesake, Daley, in the ten decathlon disciplines. Moscow was memorable for Sebastian Coe's and Steve Ovett's great tussles in the

800 metres and 1500 metres. Coe was expected to win the former and Ovett the latter but it happened the other way round. The 1500 metres took place on my birthday.

Moscow was a strange city. On one occasion we missed the press bus back to the city centre and were rescued only by the unexpected arrival of the crew from the Irish television broadcaster, RTE, whom I knew from racing and who gave us a lift. There wasn't a taxi in sight. Seoul was very different, full of the hustle and bustle of the Far East.

The biggest event of any Olympic Games is the 100 metres. I only just made it in time to see the Seoul 100 metres final, which was won by Ben Johnson who was, of course, later disqualified for taking drugs. The equestrian centre, where I was working alongside the former Olympic gold-medal-winning horseman Richard Meade, was quite a way from the centre of town and the Olympic stadium, but we were both keen to see the 100 metres. The race was due off at 2 p.m. and the break for lunch in the equestrian competition was from 1.30 to 2.15 p.m. Our taxi driver was confident we could return in time, but did not tell us that he could do this only by setting his own world record for the journey there and back. It was a close-run thing – and we almost didn't get in to the main athletics stadium. Luckily, Richard, as a gold-medal winner, had the necessary credentials to bluff our way past Security.

In fact, Seoul was an Olympics of near misses for me. I was lucky to see any of the games at all because I nearly missed my flight out. I had to cover the St Leger meeting at Doncaster before I headed East and I arrived at the airport late on Saturday for my flight. In the departure lounge I bumped into John Taylor, the former rugby player, who was covering gymnastics for ITV, and he confidently told me to follow him. Unfortunately, he had been given the wrong gate for the Seoul flight, which left us some distance from our plane at the final call. This was no problem for John, though. He could do the 100 metres in 10.2 seconds. But even for someone as athletic as D. Thompson, it would have been a close-run thing if he had been weighed down with bags of form books. John and I made it. Just. Thank goodness.

I'd be pushed to get time off these days to enjoy a third summer Olympics. It's television viewing of that for me, these days – or, should I say, video viewing – as there's plenty going on in the racing world to keep me occupied. July is one of the busiest months of the year with a full evening racing fixtures list and there's a real holiday feel to daytime meetings, especially, as you might expect, at some of the seaside courses like Yarmouth, and in the West Country for the jumping fixtures so popular with racegoers. The atmosphere is great, and at these meetings commentating can be even more fun than normal: the crowd is less serious than the average turnout at, say, the Rowley Mile course. Lots of people enjoying racing in, hopefully, sunshine.

Yarmouth is just a short drive from home and Newmarket. On a suitable summer day of fun, I took the opportunity of the lighter atmosphere to have some entertainment at Willie Ryan's expense. Willie is a fanatical Arsenal fan. He was even spotted wearing his replica kit at the Breeders' Cup in Woodbine, and rumour has it that he's slept in it, too. That day at Yarmouth was a chance to tease an Arsenal supporter in the worst way possible. I was commentating on a race in which Willie was partnering a good thing. As the horses cantered down to the start, I announced, 'The next one is Willie Ryan. Away from the races,

Willie likes nothing better than supporting his favourite football team, Tottenham Hotspur. He loves the camaraderie of watching them at their White Hart Lane ground with his mates so come on, Willie, and come on you Spurs.' Spurs are, of course, Arsenal's great North London rivals, and for Willie this was no joke. He was fuming. He won the race and later warned me, 'I'll get you back and when I do it'll be when you least expect it, in front of a million viewers.' I'm still waiting, Willie!

But racing always has a serious side to it: safety. Newmarket's July Course, the town's other racecourse across the heath from the Rowley Mile, is great fun during the holiday months. It's very relaxed, with a Sunday atmosphere. But you must never forget that jockeys risk their lives every day on the racecourse. I commentated on a race in 1996, the last on an evening card at the July Course, and the punters were cheering home Willie Carson, who was comfortably in the lead. Then the horse broke its leg. 'And Willie's down,' I said, over the public-address system, which changed the mood of the crowd completely. I kept the microphone open and when I saw Willie wave from the stretcher I put everyone at ease. But it was a reminder that, even in the nicest of locations, racing is a tough game.

Willie's fall took the edge off that evening at Newmarket. Generally speaking, though, the atmosphere on the July Course for an evening meeting is hard to beat. Walking around some racecourses feels like moving through a corridor in an office block but on the July Course, no one's pushing and it's no struggle to put a bet on. Maybe it's the steel band, Hugo and the Huguenots, that puts racegoers in such a relaxed frame of mind. I don't know. But, whatever the reason, I love it. Before racing, you can sit outside and enjoy a meal – usually seafood – if the weather's fine. A real treat.

The great thing about the racing there is that, especially during the prestigious three-day meeting in July, it's of a very high quality. You might easily see next year's Guineas winner in a maiden, or the season's eventual top two-year-old confirm the promise of an earlier maiden win in one of the juvenile Pattern races. With the two-year-old winners, you don't know if you've unearthed a Derby/Oaks type, a Guineas winner or just a future handicapper for the following year, but the horses are always a great talking point. I remember seeing Mark of Esteem and Alhaarth fight out a desperate finish on the July Course at the July Meeting in 1995. Mark of Esteem went on to win Group races aplenty at three, including the 2000 Guineas, and Alhaarth was ultimately rated the top juvenile of his generation and won a Group race at Longchamp at three. Sayyedati, who won the Jacques Le Marois and Sussex Stakes as well as the 1000 Guineas, was another July Course winner. She was brilliant at two in the Cherry Hinton. Juveniles thrive in the relaxed atmosphere, the ground is always well watered and the July Course doesn't have as severe a dip as the Rowley Mile in the last furlong running to the line, which makes the race a gentle test for harder races to come.

The July meeting is truly international. A lot of Americans are in town and the Japanese are an increasing presence. I interviewed a delegation from Japan for Channel 4 one year through an interpreter from the Japanese Racing Association and had to keep reminding myself to direct my questions to the JRA man, not the delegation's head.

All Europe's main players come to Newmarket for the July Meeting, too. The Head family is always strongly represented: I interviewed Criquette a few moments before Anabaa won the July Cup for her in 1996 and we were interrupted by her father Alec, himself a great trainer, when Criquette spoke of her season so far. 'Only fifty-five winners?' teased Alec. 'Is that all?' Alec's son, Freddie, was in the saddle for Anabaa's success. Freddie has taken a lot of criticism for some of his rides over the years and after Anabaa had sprinted to victory Freddie joked, 'Another bad race in the July Cup, I suppose.' I'm sure he would admit to having deserved some of the stick he has taken in the past, but he has been at the top for so long, which is surely sufficient proof of his genuine ability. Freddie has also been French champion jockey many times, further testimony to his talent.

With such cosmopolitan visitors, Newmarket is a great place to stay – and live – in July. Many of the town's trainers, jockeys and established bloodstock figures have cocktail parties and barbecues. It's very sociable. The entertaining extends to the racecourse, too, and it's well worth planning a stopover for an evening fixture if you make the journey. The Friday and Saturday evening meetings are now very much part of the racing calendar and afterwards there's usually a band, like Showaddywaddy or Suzi Quatro, playing to a crowd – in front of the Jockey Club Stand, of all places. The music started a few years ago and it's possibly the last place on earth you would expect to go to hear Marty Wilde and the Wilde Cats or Gerry and the Pacemakers. Still, it's great. You can take along a bottle of wine. It's a late finish for racing people but plenty stay up for it. Come and see for yourself.

Near the end of the month, a lot of the town's big trainers leave Newmarket for a few days 'shopping' at the Keeneland yearling sales and the televised racing may give up-and-coming trainers, serving time as assistants before starting up on their own, an opportunity to enjoy some early limelight, or trusted head lads to take a bow on screen. It can be tricky for them: they don't want to say anything wrong in case they upset the boss. Anyway, most of them are much more at ease in the pub on a Saturday night. But I know what it's like to do the assistant's job from my time with Denys Smith. I try to remember that and give those who deserve one a rare plug. Nowadays, assistant trainers can win a working holiday abroad, financed by the memorial fund set up to commemorate the late Alex Scott, who was so tragically murdered. We did a piece about the fund on Channel 4, which I hope meant more people got to know about the chance to learn training methods abroad before embarking on a career in Newmarket, Lambourn, or in the north.

Away from Newmarket in July, the relaxed atmosphere colours the calendar, especially in the south. Sandown and its Eclipse Stakes day is hugely popular with locals and Londoners, particularly those who live south of the Thames. The Eclipse is usually on the first Saturday of July. At the end of the month, it's Goodwood and five days of high-quality racing. There's no shortage of excellent racing entertainment in the south at the beginning and end of July, as well as in the middle.

I miss out on a lot of the fun of Sandown and the Eclipse. It's quite a boozy day and I'm driving home so no drink for me. I'm also in the winner's enclosure next to the paddock so I'm the wrong side of the grandstand for the live drama of the finish. But I'm not complaining: I get paid to go to one of the best races of the year, I don't have to buy a badge and I have the run of the racecourse. I know all the gatemen now and they make me feel more than at home. In return, it's my job to make those who haven't made the journey wish they had and help explain what is going on to new viewers who might be watching racing for the first time so they'll watch again.

By comparison with Sandown, Goodwood isn't a favourite of mine, though I can see its popularity from the huge crowds that attend each of the five 'Glorious' days. The landscape is certainly beautiful, but I don't know. It's just not my favourite place. Even when I worked at Goodwood for BBC radio, the atmosphere always left me a bit cold. Maybe it's because at heart I'm a northerner. Whatever the reason, I never look forward to commentating at Goodwood, or the three-hour drive home to Newmarket.

What can be great about Goodwood is the opportunity it offers for punting. By the time of the Glorious Goodwood meeting, the form for the season has just about stabilized with the consistent, firm summer ground. Everyone loves a winner at the races, and if it has been a dry summer, it can be easier to pick one at Goodwood.

The winners may be harder to unearth in Ireland, but I have none of the reservations about racing there that I have about Goodwood. It's just a pity that I don't manage to travel over as often as I would like for the big races like the Irish Derby, the high spot of July's racing in the Emerald Isle. Julie loves going to Ireland, too. The problem is that a lot of the best racing that we screen clashes with other big events in Britain also covered by Channel 4. We have a lot of viewers in Ireland and we use the RTE coverage for the big races with Robert Hall and Ted Walsh doing the honours, accompanied by the commentary of Tony O'Hehir.

The Morning Line is especially popular in Ireland. I found this out on a day trip to Tralee. Gerry Crean runs the Green Man pub in Six Mile Bottom near Newmarket. His family also owns Tralee. On a trip there with Gerry, and Tony Elves, the *Sporting Life*'s Newmarket man, we flew to Shannon airport where we picked up a hire car. It was fine up to that point, but then things started to go wrong. Tony had got word of a real certainty that afternoon, so on the two-hour drive to the racecourse we kept a look-out for a betting shop and found one in a small village somewhere in the west of Ireland. Sure enough, the horse bolted in at 7–1. The only snag was that Gerry and Tony had put quite a bit on, which left the shop on its knees and the owner none too happy. It was not looking good. Luckily, some of the lads in the shop recognized me as 'that guy on the telly' so I chatted away to them about an imaginary Newmarket flyer while Gerry and Tony negotiated their payout and got the engine running. 'Mention us on *The Morning Line*,' the lads shouted, as we made a swift exit. On balance, the deal seemed a good one and I was happy to oblige soon afterwards.

The Irish Derby is the biggest occasion that we share with RTE on Channel 4. With the tremendous atmosphere at the Curragh on Derby Day it really brings the three-year-old season alive. Recently St Jovite and Balanchine stick in the mind. St Jovite was brilliant in 1992, just awesome. Two years later Balanchine confirmed the arrival of the Godolphin team as a major force in British and world racing: as the filly had wintered in Dubai as a two-year-old, and also won the Epsom Oaks. I remember doing a review of the 1994 season and used footage of Frankie Dettori jumping off the filly at the Curragh and hugging Sheikh Mohammed. It's great to see owners get involved. It's like Cheltenham, but on the flat it's usually some of the most powerful men in the world.

It's amazing how a horse can improve between Epsom and the Curragh. Horses out of the frame at Epsom can be right back in the reckoning for the Irish

Derby. The wide-open galloping Curragh track can transform a horse who has disappointed at Epsom. But, ultimately, if a horse runs well at Epsom, it's pretty sure to perform at the Curragh. If it's good enough to handle the undulations of Epsom Downs then it will have the ability to reproduce the form in Ireland.

In recent years Zagreb was one of the best Irish Derby winners. He demolished a top-class field in 1996 to give his trainer Dermot Weld a first success in the race. Dermot is at the top of his profession and is following in the great tradition of Irish trainers like Paddy Prendergast and, of course, Vincent O'Brien. Dermot Weld is always searching for ways to give his horses an edge. For example, no one is allowed to shout in Dermot's yard, the horses must have calm. He made history by sending Go And Go to win the Belmont Stakes, the third leg of the US Triple Crown at Belmont Park in New York. He also saddled Vintage Crop to win the Melbourne Cup, an unbelievable achievement. Imagine taking the risk of flying a horse of Vintage Crop's calibre half-way round the world to compete in a race that had never been won by a European-trained runner. Dermot is always looking for new challenges and new frontiers. He's pretty proud of Vintage Crop, who spent a winter in Dubai recuperating from injury. When I visited Dermot's yard for *The Morning Line* a few years ago, to film an Irish Derby Day feature, he modestly claimed at first that he couldn't find the video of Vintage Crop winning in Australia. Then it was suddenly in the machine and pictures of the race were on the screen. Twenty-three plays and two hours later we left!

Aidan O'Brien is the coming man. Success for his stable in the 1997 Irish 1000 and 2000 Guineas is proof of that. If you look at him you might think he worked in an optician's selling glasses, or was an accountant, but he had smashed all records for training winners in Ireland on the flat and over jumps. It's only a matter of time before he starts to dominate the big races in Britain, too. He has already won the Whitbread Gold Cup with Life Of A Lord in 1996. I think that big-race success on the mainland was the first of many.

Another recent success story from Ireland is Johnny Murtagh, a very underrated jockey. I've got to know him well from spending time with him in Dubai. I remember playing golf there with him once and he kept teasing me about what his mother would say when he told her he'd played golf with Derek Thompson. After that he rode Ridgewood Pearl to win the Breeders' Cup Mile, as well as some other big races, and became champion jockey in Ireland. When I next saw him I said that when we next played golf again it would be my mother who was impressed. Johnny had terrible weight problems and went off the rails when he was an apprentice. His wife, Ula, has been very supportive in helping him sort everything out and making him the jockey he is today. His weight is still a real bind, though. When we go out to dinner in Dubai he sometimes has just a glass of water, even though he's starving and we're all having great food and wine. It was great when he won the Breeders' Cup, and also when he took the Coronation Stakes at Royal Ascot. That was Ridgewood Pearl again. Johnny had been telling anybody who would listen – and a few who wouldn't – that she was a great filly. He came into the winners' enclosure shouting to anyone, 'I told you so, I told you so.' There isn't an ounce of spare flesh on Johnny , and he has this tremendous rapport with horses, which is a real gift, and he's so strong in a finish.

It's great when the winners of the Epsom and the

Irish Derby meet the older horses in the King George VI and Queen Elizabeth Diamond Stakes at Ascot to round off July. Professionally, the race doesn't register much with me because I'm usually working elsewhere for Channel 4, and Ascot is a BBC track, but I was thrilled for Michael Hills, another jockey I got to know really well in Dubai, when he won the race on Pentire. Michael has been a good mate. He was beaten on Pentire in 1995 and was criticized for going too early against Lammtarra, but he set the record straight a year later. With his Australian wife, Chrissy, I watched him win the 1996 Epsom Derby on Shaamit, the month before he won the King George. A few days after he completed the double they popped into a pub where Julie and I were having a snack and we had a great night. Great company in a great racing month.

AUGUST

Grand Old York

I was born in County Durham, but I'm an adopted Yorkshireman. As with all Yorkshiremen, a York-shireman first and an Englishman second. I may have been born on the wrong side of the river to be eligible to play cricket for the county, but I lived in Yorkshire for twenty years, more than long enough for it to become my adopted spiritual home, which it remains even though today I live in Newmarket.

This alone would probably be enough to make York's Ebor meeting in August the highlight of my racing year. Anyone from Yorkshire who follows racing is proud of York. But there are plenty of other reasons, too, as well as pride in the Knavesmire race-course. There is the quality of the racing, of course, but there are also the personalities associated with the Knavesmire and the great atmosphere of the three-day meeting. Although it can sometimes be uncomfortably hot in the commentary box or in front of camera, it's always a memorable week.

The Ebor meeting is very different from the Dante meeting in May at the same track: the August event is an occasion with something for everyone. I think my ideal holiday would be two weeks of the racing at York in August, if they could stage that many days' running and keep up the high quality. (I'm sure they could!) It's real value for money, too, compared with, say, Ascot. Champagne at York won't set you back the earth. They say it's the Ascot of the north. Maybe, on second thoughts, Ascot is the York of the south.

My mother, Lillian, lives about an hour away from York, at Nunthorpe, which means I sometimes stay with her instead of at the Mount Royal, my usual stopover for this venue. She's not a big critic of me professionally, my mum, but she does ring up to tell me if I'm looking a bit pale on the screen. 'You're a bit peaky,' she might say. I think she enjoys seeing me on television: it means she can keep an eye on me.

By the middle of August the Classic races are all but over and you might not see too many rematches of some of the great finishes from earlier in the season over the same trips – there is no chance of Entrepreneur and Revoque clashing again over one mile as they did in the 1997 2000 Guineas. But the older horses come up against the three-year-olds, in some cases for the first time, and the York meeting has its great handicaps as well as its own championship contests, like the old Benson and Hedges Gold Cup.

I tipped Roberto at 12–1 to beat Brigadier Gerard and win the first running of the B & H, which is now called the International. In 1972, when it was first staged, it was a new style of race, over an extended ten furlongs. Today, races over the same distance have really come into their own. Ten furlongs is today's global trip. Horses like Halling, who won the International twice, in 1995 and 1996, are true specialists, and if you breed one as good as him you can try to prove he's the best in Europe over the distance, and then in the world by running on dirt in the Breeders'

Cup Classic and the Dubai World Cup.

The Ebor Handicap, on the middle Wednesday of the three days, has a huge following, especially among the northern racing set. For many owners, trainers and jockeys, it's the highlight of the week with all the race's history and tradition. I sometimes feel that the winner of the Ebor doesn't get the recognition that the feat deserves, which is a shame, and that perhaps the main reason for this is that it is not a Pattern race, so the winner does not earn 'black type'. The Pattern system, which is internationally recognized, grades the best races of the year as Group One, Two, Three or Listed. These races, which are assessed by the Pattern Committees of major racing nations, carry the kudos of the Pattern's black type. By winning a black-type race you have a level of performance that is internationally recognized. Owners try to earn black-type status on the racecourse, as a horse with it stands out to international buyers in a sales catalogue and, consequently, is more likely to make a good price in the auction ring.

I think that success in the Ebor warrants some kind of official, black-type recognition. Even if the winner carries only seven stone twelve pounds, it has to be a good handicapper to earn the right to run in the race in the first place. Handicaps in America carry black type. Why not in Britain? The Pattern system is universally accepted as an indicator of quality and, these days, the bloodstock market is so international. The serious consequences for home racegoers, though, is that some of the better horses trained in Britain end up running on the mainland in Europe where races, which don't take as much winning as the Ebor, carry black type. I know that we're all Europeans now, but I still hate interviewing a winning trainer who says his horse is going to run in a race in Belgium to try to win some black type. The Pattern system is a mess. Surely winning a competitive handicap like the Ebor is a greater achievement than winning some of the Group Three races in, say, Germany?

At least York's juvenile races are afforded the recognition they deserve – and so they should be. A juvenile winner at York is usually good enough to contest the year's two-year-old championship events later in the year and, hopefully, the Classics at Newmarket, Epsom and Doncaster at three. York's two-year-old races are reason enough for making a trip to the Knavesmire. The juveniles are just that bit more mature than June's Royal Ascot two-year-olds and have sometimes strengthened up or improved on early-season runs. In August, they're ready to begin to show their true abilities. Abou Zouz, who won the 1996 Gimcrack Stakes, is a good example. He was a lovely yearling. I remember being asked by one of Sheikh Mohammed's team what I thought of him before he was sold at public auction at Tattersalls. I reckoned he would make at least fifty thousand guineas and he was eventually sold to Wafic Said for over three hundred thousand. But Abou Zouz had been beaten on his first two outings as a juvenile – at Newmarket's Guineas meeting and then at Kempton. It took until August and York for the horse to come right for his trainer, David Loder, who also struggled at the beginning of the 1996 season before running into a great patch of form later in the year. I tipped Abou Zouz to win at York, on the strength of what I had seen in the sales ring the year before. It was obvious that he had great potential and those defeats hadn't changed my mind.

I suppose the one complaint I have about the Ebor meeting is that I never have the chance to speak to any of my friends there. It's exactly the sort of occasion that makes working in racing such a pleasure and also so frustrating! There's a real buzz about the place, but work commitments have to come first. The ladies make a real effort to look their best and brighten up the place, too, which makes missing out on the fun even more irritating. Clement Freud, who writes a column in the *Sporting Life*, commented once that the women at York were built like second-row rugby forwards. Well, he's wrong – and he's lucky the racecourse let him come back after that.

I think that it's the great mix of racing stars and celebrities from other walks of life, especially football, which makes York and its Ebor meeting so special. From the racing world, Mick and Peter Easterby, Yorkshiremen through and through, are a great pair. Mick – known as 'Spitting Mick' – is the only man who has spat on air while I've been interviewing him. Think of Peter, and Sea Pigeon springs to mind straight away. What a pity that ITV was on strike in 1979, the year that Sea Pigeon won the Ebor as there's no footage of it. Two completely different York characters, but no less compelling for it, are Lord Manton and Lord Hartington. They are both York regulars and sit on the racing committee. Manton is a classic English gentleman: he did everyone a big favour by employing John Smith as clerk of the course at York. Hartington, whose father is the colourful Duke of Devonshire, is also the former Senior Steward to the Jockey Club and was the first chairman of the British Horseracing Board.

From the world of football, Geoff Hurst, whom everyone knows scored a hat-trick in the World Cup final for England in 1966, is a regular, and Bryan Robson used to come every year when he was still playing. My brother once rang to tell me that Robbo, who by this time was manager at Middlesbrough, had gone to Brazil to buy Juninho, but I had to tell him that

I had left Robbo in the pub half an hour before the telephone call. In fact, he flew out the next day. Jack Charlton, one of Bryan's predecessors at Middlesbrough, also likes to come to York. I got to know Big Jack quite well from his time at 'Boro. He caught me out one year at the Knavesmire when he asked me for an autograph. I felt a right idiot when I looked up and saw who it was. He was one of the most relaxed football managers I've ever met. He was laid back at the races, too. 'I just like being one of the crowd,' he said. 'I don't want to be in a hospitality box or anything like that. I'm here to have a good day out with the missus and some mates.' The Yorkshire crowd love him. He was a great Leeds player in the sixties and seventies, and was instrumental in bringing much success to the club. And, of course, he played alongside Geoff Hurst in the World Cup final.

The two sides to York – the celebrity crowd and the racing crowd – come together for the Gimcrack dinner later in the year. This occasion is meant to celebrate racing in general and also to recognize the winner of that year's Gimcrack Stakes. The winning Gimcrack owner is invited to make a speech to a distinguished guest list and someone replies on behalf of the sport. I've been lucky enough to attend a few Gimcrack dinners, including one where Cliff Morgan, the great rugby commentator, was a guest speaker. At the time, I was working for Radio 2 and Cliff was my boss, the head of sport. When I bumped into him he asked me what I was doing at the dinner. I pointed out that it was more unusual for him to be at a racing occasion. In his address, he reminded everyone that I had once tipped him a horse who had fallen in the paddock at Perth (it tripped). Thanks, Cliff.

I think, though, that there's one real celebrity who sums up the warm, friendly atmosphere at York. He's the security officer who makes sure that a path is cleared for the winner and placed horses to walk into the winner's enclosure. He's the young lad, I think in his twenties, who shouts, 'Stand back, stand back!' I interviewed him once on Channel 4. You'll have heard him in the background on television crying, 'Mind your backs! This one'll run you over.' I reckon he's more famous than anyone else on the racecourse.

Every day, sadly, cannot be York and the Ebor meeting, but Channel 4's racing team is kept busy throughout the month with 'bread and butter' – for want of a better phrase – racing at Sandown and Newmarket, and the evening racing season is still in full swing. If the latter is not being screened by Sky and its *Winning Post* team then I might be asked to commentate for SIS. I still get a little uptight for these meetings, be they for Channel 4, SIS or just the racecourse crowd, even if the racing doesn't receive the same billing as the quality cards of York in August. Mel Fordham, a Newmarket-based racecourse photographer, once saw me before a home meeting. He said, 'You still get nervous before going on air, don't you? Even after all these times you've appeared.' He's right.

I think there might be too much racing in August. Bank holidays can feature as many as sixteen meetings, which is dangerously close to spreading the horse population too thin. Nobody wants small fields and that's sometimes what we end up with nationwide. But, having said that, some of the smaller tracks enjoy their biggest gates on bank holidays.

The Radio 5 Live team does a marvellous job on bank holidays when there are so many meetings to monitor. Racing has really fought its corner on the new sport and news channel – full marks to Cornelius Lysaght, the racing reporter, for developing his role. The station seems packed full of racing previews and provides excellent coverage of the events as they happen, and a lot of the credit must be due to him. John Inverdale is another on Radio 5 who gives racing a good airing. He is one of a rare breed: an excellent general all-round broadcaster, who really knows his horses. These two top professionals make up for the amateurs like David Mellor. Mellor, the former MP for Putney who lost his seat in the 1997 election, has hosted the football phone-in programme, *606*. When one of his shows also featured the Breeders' Cup races live from across the Atlantic he had the cheek to tell listeners not to go away when the broadcast went over to Woodbine for commentary on the racing because the 'great thing about racing is that it's over very quickly'. I can't believe he got away with that. I remember when I once told viewers that the adverts were coming up so there was time to make a cup of tea. The producers went mad, and rightly so, as without the adverts there would be fewer Channel 4 racing broadcasts. I hope David Mellor received a dressing down. He deserved it.

Bank holidays on Channel 4 take me back to the days of the ITV Seven. Often the quality of racing for an ITV Seven was poor so we would pack the programme full of action. The punters watching at home loved it. For them, you can't beat big fields, close finishes and generously priced winners. Great television.

If the racing is lacking something, a novelty element can enhance it: for example, the Moët & Chandon Amateurs' Derby at Epsom on August Bank Holiday lifts the overall card for television. The race has a field of amateur jockeys from all over Europe with whom the viewers are not familiar so there are bound to be plenty of stories to tell about the riders and their backgrounds. The jockey who rode the winner in 1996 of this important amateur event is a case in point. Lord Huntingdon's Arabian Story was successfully part-nered by young Luis Urbano. Viewers from the sixties and seventies will remember the winning jockey's father, also Luis, who used to travel from his native Spain to ride in Britain. For me, it was extra special. I can remember the young Urbano as a lad swimming at his father's pool in Spain. He was tall even then, com-pared with his stocky, strong dad, but he still made up into a useful rider.

I came across Luis in the eighties when I was in Spain with Willie Shoemaker and some of the top jockeys of the time. Willie, or Bill as a lot of his friends call him, was on a worldwide farewell tour so I arranged for him to ride in Madrid in a jockeys' chal-lenge against the likes of Greville Starkey and Tony Ives, who have now retired, and Richard Quinn and John Reid who are still riding brilliantly today. Apart from the press conference, when Bill was asked questions in Spanish which he didn't speak, every-thing went well before the event and there were ten thousand at the track for the race. Greville caught his foot on a nail sticking out from a running rail, which costs him some good rides in the weeks that followed, but other than that it was a great success. It just goes to show that you can make any racing great entertain-ment, which is, after all, what it's all about. The jockeys weren't riding great horses, but it still held the public's attention.

A good-priced touch is also great television. Newmarket's August meetings can throw up one or two, which gets Big Mac going about the day's 'steamer', as the early-morning price of an afternoon's runner shortens with the bookmakers while we're on air. At this time of year, you hear plans being made on the Newmarket gallops on the Wednesday for Friday and Saturday's racing. It's well worth the early start to observe trainers putting horses through their paces, and I'll get up and head to the Newmarket heath without even a shave to see one being prepared for a really nice touch on the July Course a few days later. And it doesn't have to end there. I once interviewed Conrad Allen, one of Newmarket's most enterprising trainers, after a winner on a Newmarket Saturday and he told me, bullish as anything, that the horse would run on Monday again 'and win', and on Thursday and Saturday, too. His confidence was not misplaced.

Some credit for a Newmarket winner must always go to Peter Amos, who is general manager of the Jockey Club Estates and looks after the town's all-weather and turf gallops. Peter is proud of every home success and records all Newmarket's winners – about a thousand in a season – in a big book. He's pretty sharp. When gypsies camped on racecourse-owned land, next to the July Course, during the summer racing he was quick to lay some 'essential' fertilizer and manure up-wind of them. The first blustery day and, before the next meeting, they were on their way.

Peter Player is the other Peter who keeps Newmarket at the forefront of the racing world. He is the innovative chairman of Newmarket racecourse. Take the possibility of an all-weather racecourse in the town to go with the Rowley Mile and the July Course and provide fixtures during the winter: most traditionalists said, straight away, no, it would interfere with the gallops. Others, more open-minded to change, gave it some consideration but ultimately concluded that it wouldn't work without an indoor viewing area to protect racegoers from the cold, which at Newmarket can be severe. But Peter Player maintained that the town should at least look at plans for a scheme before rejecting it. I think his attitude is right:

in my book, 'why not' is a better way to look at things than 'why'.

I believe in the way Peter considers new developments because racing should always be looking to make itself more attractive to the public. Racing has always changed and evolved. It needs people all over the world to share Peter's visionary approach to see the possibilities for racing on the international stage. We take international racing for granted today: it seems perfectly natural for a trainer to nominate the Breeders' Cup or the Japan Cup as the target for a horse who has just won a big race at York or Epsom. Horses are flown all around the world to run in races like the Melbourne Cup, which attracts a cosmopolitan field. But owners, trainers and racecourse management had to be open to the idea.

The Washington International was the forerunner to jet-set racing. In 1968 Sir Ivor made the journey across the Atlantic to Washington DC for what was then a mile and a half race, run in the fall. I remember making the trip to Laurel racecourse to see Dahlia, the brilliant French mare, whom Lester Piggott rode in 1973 to win her second King George VI and Queen Elizabeth Diamond Stakes. I went with my father and got up at 5 a.m. to see the horses work on the track. At the time, I thought there would be more races like this, bringing the best horses in the world together. Lester was the first truly international jockey. The Americans could not believe his riding style, with the short stirrups and his bottom in the air, but he won so many races that he had the last laugh.

The international season for Europe-based trainers really begins in August with the Arlington Million in Chicago. It's commonplace now for a trainer to send a horse over from Britain as the purse is so good. In 1985 Teleprompter showed everyone it was possible to win round Arlington, a typically tight US track for a European runner, and since him, others have followed. In 1984 John Henry, the world-record-breaking American gelding, had won, so Teleprompter was keeping good company.

Teleprompter was trained in Richmond, Yorkshire, by Bill Watts, who used to gallop his string on the old local racecourse, which still had a judge's box overlooking where the finish line used to be. Bill believed it was feasible for a smaller stable to fly out a runner for the Arlington Million and had the courage to go for it. He also had the support of the horse's owner, Lord Derby. Teleprompter was all heart. After he had been retired from racing he used to lead the two-year-olds up the gallops and if one got past him it was usually a good one. At the time of his Arlington Million win, I lived about five miles away from the yard, so the victory was really special. There were plenty of local celebrations, including a 'Welcome home, Teleprompter' party. I did a programme for Yorkshire Television about the impact Teleprompter and the Million win had had on the area and we finished by interviewing an old man, who said, 'He made my day.' That summed it up. Tony Ives rode Teleprompter at Arlington. Willie Carson, who usually rode for the horse's owner, apparently called the horse an 'old boat' after he was beaten in a race, but I reckon he changed his mind after the Million.

Closer to home in August, but still international in character, is Deauville. Some people compare it to York as it's so relaxed, but it's a different 'relaxed' from York 'relaxed'. Deauville is a holiday town but some of the horses are trained on the beach. It's also very glamorous. Cash Asmussen was king of Deauville when he was champion jockey in France. Every night he ate at the same top restaurant. Recently

I filmed a Channel 4 piece along the Deauville promenade to go with a recording of the Prix Jacques Le Marois, the big race of the month. I interviewed the head waiter at Cash's restaurant, who pointed out the tables reserved over the years by the Prince Aly Khan and Elizabeth Taylor.

Now Cash is no longer king in Deauville: Olivier Peslier has taken over. I always refer to him as the Frankie Dettori of France. In 1996 he proved himself a jockey of the same calibre by winning the Prix de l'Arc de Triomphe on Helissio. Olivier's wife, Marie, works for a French television station, which broadcasts racing. I interviewed her on *The Morning Line* before Entrepreneur's 2000 Guineas success and Marie tipped her husband's mount, Zamindar, in the race, as well as success for the French-trained Pas de Réponse in the following day's 1000 Guineas. Her loyal – and patriotic – selections were not quite good enough, fifth and fourth respectively, but Olivier will have a string of English Classic wins before he retires.

Both Deauville and the Million used to be screened by Channel 4 and I miss the prospect of a trip to Deauville or Arlington in August to cover top-quality racing on the world stage, but in racing, you never know what the future holds, and I hope to go back to these places some day in a professional capacity. At least until then there will always be York and its Ebor meeting.

SEPTEMBER

Donny, Dettori and David Vine

The month of September will probably never be the same again for Frankie Dettori, Ascot racecourse, racing – and the world of sport, for that matter. At the end of the month Ascot stages some of the best races of the season as part of its Festival meeting. It was conceived in 1987 as a showpiece occasion for the whole industry, a chance to show the public how exciting racing can be by staging high-quality cards featuring everything good about the game. But now, regardless of who's running or how attractive the day's card is to the punter or racegoer, everyone will always remember the day in September 1996 when Frankie went through the seven-race card: his Magnificent Seven.

The first time I met Frankie, he was an apprentice, albeit a promising one, with Luca Cumani. I had heard from someone in Newmarket that a young jockey in town was improving his riding style by practising on a mechanical horse. I thought it was worth finding out who he was as I felt his training regime might make a good piece for Channel 4. It was Frankie – and it did.

During filming of the mechanical horse piece, Frankie encouraged me to have a go on it. In one minute I was exhausted. Frankie said that he rode it to music for half an hour. It was then that I realized he was a jockey dedicated enough to make it all the way to the top – and fit! Today, you can spot him around Newmarket in his sweat suit and baseball cap in the middle of a run that might be as long as nine miles. I bumped into him once at the bottom of Warren Hill and tried to encourage him to jog up it. 'Tommo, you mad?' he asked. Nine miles on the level is fine, but Frankie always likes to keep enough up his sleeve for the next tight finish.

We've had our moments, Frankie and I. At one time, he was refusing to speak to the press, and I ended up at a dinner table with him and a few others as guests of Willie Ryan. Frankie turned to Willie and asked what was going on as I was press. Willie was quick to tell him that I was a friend of his. After all, Willie was best man at my wedding. Nevertheless, when Frankie and I bumped into each other later in the gents' we ended up having a real, ding-dong argument about the coverage he had received in the media, which had prompted his silence. Our exchange seemed to last hours, but I think, in some respects, it cleared the air. Now we are the best of friends.

I wasn't commentating the day Frankie went through the card at Ascot as it is a BBC racecourse – but I was there! My personal insight into the day came a few weeks later when I interviewed Frankie about it for a special commemorative video. On the evening of his seven-timer, Jamie Hawksfield, with whom I work on a number of racing videos every year, rang me and said that we should do something with Frankie about his historic day. This was set up pretty quickly the following morning. I interviewed Frankie for nearly four hours. He was brilliant. 'I know you're good at these things,' I said, 'but you're on fire today. You're giving us such great material.'

'I don't want to forget anything,' he explained. 'I want everything down on tape so I have something for my grandchildren.'

During filming, Frankie revealed that before racing at Ascot that Saturday, he reckoned that he had a chance of three, maybe four winners on the day. But no more than that. Before the second race, in which he partnered Diffident for Godolphin, Frankie said to the yard's head lad, John Davies, that if he won he would walk naked round the Newmarket clock tower at the top of the high street. John said he would, too. Well, we're still waiting!

The interview was fascinating. Frankie remembered where every horse was for all seven races. He talked me through Mark of Esteem's stunning win in the Group One Queen Elizabeth II Mile and the point in the race when he thought, 'Hey, I should be going now.' How he nearly fell off the back when the horse accelerated, having been swinging off the bridle only moments before. How the crowd went ballistic. In the sixth race, he rode Lochangel for Ian Balding, who had told him to hold the horse up off the pace. Frankie thought he would get torn off a strip for leading all the way. In the last race, Fujiyama Crest went off at 2–1. I remember thinking on the day, with the big weight it was carrying, that the horse was at least a 10–1 shot, even though he had won the race the year before, but with a little less lead in the saddle. I couldn't believe the sort of money that must have been gambled on Frankie to land a seventh race for his mount to start at such odds. The video captures all of this, and the pressure Frankie was under with all that money riding on his last mount.

For Frankie, I think the day was so special because his father, Gianfranco, a Classic winner in his own right as a jockey, had ridden six winners in a single day during his own career but never seven. Apparently Gianfranco, who was abroad and missed the day, flashed up the Ceefax to see how Frankie had done and thought that there must be some error on the information service.

I think the 'Magnificent Seven' video is one of the best in which I've been involved. When I took a copy into the weighing room at Newmarket to show Frankie, he was enjoying a glass of champagne after having ridden a treble. 'A bad day today,' he joked. 'Only three winners.' He also asked me how much I was paid for my work filming. When I kidded him that I received as much as he did – definitely not true – he complained, 'But I did all the work!'

I suppose everyone has their own special Frankie story, and I'm no different. I remember at York, one day, Frankie threw his whip from the saddle as he was led into the winner's enclosure. It went straight through the open weighing-room window from about fifteen yards away. Take my word for it, it was quite a feat. What a great guy. In twenty years' time, he could have put even Lester Piggott in the shade, and he has all the personality to go with his great skills as a jockey.

The Ascot Festival, which has become a two-day weekend fixture, is a great occasion. Its development as a showpiece for the sport has been handicapped by wet weather, which has hit its crowds badly, but the racing is top quality and Frankie's great feat might well be the making of it if people can be persuaded to come without expecting him to do it every year. The racecourse is certainly playing its part in making the day such a success: Ascot is rapidly losing its reputation for stuffiness and even the gate men, with their bowler hats, are less formidable now. In recent years Douglas Erskine-Crum, the racecourse director, and

Nick Cheyne, the clerk of the course, have really turned the place round. A few years ago, you would never have expected to see racecourse security men asking for autographs, but that's what happened on the Sunday after Frankie's Magnificent Seven.

As well as Frankie's achievements, Mark of Esteem's success in the Queen Elizabeth II Mile in 1996 was a boost to the meeting. It provided the Saturday crowd that year, which had a fair sprinkling of first-time race-goers, with a racing high spot – and gave me a lot of pleasure, too: Mark of Esteem was my winning nap of the day. Simon Crisford had said that the Godolphin horse was in better condition than he had been before he won the 2000 Guineas at Newmarket in May. I had also seen Bosra Sham, the main rival in the race, being walked at the bottom of Warren Hill. Her trainer, Henry Cecil, didn't seem confident enough about her feet, which had given her trouble all season, to work her, and that cleared the way for Mark of Esteem to run away with the race, which he did.

The BBC is doing its best to build up the Ascot Festival and make it the centrepiece of *Grandstand* on both the Saturday and Sunday programmes. BBC Sport's Sue Barker, the former tennis player, has been used as the link between the racing world and the sporting public, who make up the majority of the *Grandstand* audience. To go from a tennis professional to the top of sports broadcasting, covering all events and not just her own specialist discipline, is a great achievement. She understands the pressures of sport at the highest level, which can help when interviewing competitors and explaining to viewers what a particular moment means. My strength is journalism, and the excellent grounding I received in radio broadcasting. It compensates for my tennis: when I play John Francome, he has the doubles tram-lines as extra ground to cover and I have just a singles court! That way I don't lose too easily.

Unlike the Ascot Festival the St Leger is well established. For me, it doesn't need building up at all. At the beginning of September, I still have butterflies in my stomach when I arrive at Doncaster on St Leger day. The race is British racing's oldest Classic. It is part of racing history and one of my favourite racing occasions – in September and the whole racing year.

I also have great memories of Doncaster because it's where I met Julie. I was interviewing someone on the Friday before the St Leger – I forget who! – when I saw her out the corner of my eye. Well. The conversation I was supposed to be having for the benefit of the viewers and the programme dried up and I didn't even notice the on-air pause. I wasn't concentrating on work. I persuaded the floor manager to take a note to Julie asking her to have dinner with me. He did, and thought that she had agreed, but in fact she had said no. Knowing Julie as I do now, I realize that the request should have been delivered by me in person to have had any chance of being accepted.

At the time, she had no idea who I was. She had just moved to Doncaster and it was her first visit to the racecourse. Her mother, Mary Summerfield, was with her and explained that I was on television. (I learned later that her father, Syd Summerfield, a big racing fan, knew of me, too, but used to turn the sound down when I was on.) Mary's information about my identity was only so helpful, though: Julie thought I was David Vine! I suppose I can see what she meant – I wore glasses then. But David is a bit older than me and I'm not sure I looked over fifty at the time.

The floor manager's misunderstanding of what had happened when he had given Julie the note was not very helpful, either. I thought I was all set to have din-

ner with her so when I was off air and went over to
thank her, and make an arrangement, I was surprised
to learn that she hadn't been satisfied with the note.
She was eventually persuaded after I had made my
apologies and asked her again, this time face to face.
We went to the Old Vienna restaurant, to which we
now return each St Leger. We were both married when
we met, which made things difficult. It did not help
either that Joe Mercer, the former jockey, and Jimmy
Scott, Michael Stoute's travelling head lad, just happened to be in the restaurant that night.

The following day, Saturday, Minster Son won the
St Leger for Willie Carson, Neil Graham and Lady
Beaverbrook. Neil Graham had taken over training the
horse from Major Dick Hern, who was ill. Willie had
also bred the colt, who is now at stud. After the race I
left for the Olympics in Seoul and was away for about
eight weeks. Julie tells me now that she thought, Well,
that's it. The situation was complicated, not least by
outside pressures, with me being on television. When
I got back, we were stalked by the newspapers, which
tracked me down at Ayr. It was easy for the tabloid
journalists because they always knew from the racing
calendar where I was going to be. Some even booked
into the room next to mine in a hotel where I was
staying. Julie's husband, Charles, was traced to the
hospital where he worked, and people we both knew
were being offered five-figure sums to spill the beans.
It was horrible. Bob Champion has experienced it, too.
It's so unfair to everyone involved, especially the
children. Thank goodness everything worked out for
all concerned.

Even so, I have only good memories of Doncaster
and the St Leger meeting, which runs from Wednesday to Saturday, with great racing, and the Doncaster
bloodstock sales taking place nearby. When I was a

kid, Doncaster seemed a million miles away from Stockton, even though it's hardly any distance at all.

There's definitely a different atmosphere at Doncaster, especially for the St Leger. Its mining-community roots have something to do with it. People have a local pride in the race and come to watch it because they're Yorkshire folk, born and bred. At York it's more a case of 'see and be seen'. People dress up for the St Leger for their own enjoyment rather than to be noticed. Nothing too fancy, though. I don't think the Doncaster ladies are prepared to spend a fortune on clothes. Clement Freud – him again – once described them as having no intelligence, nothing to say and being built like battleships. Well, we had some on the programme, organized by Julie, which proved otherwise – and it probably got a few extra fellas through the gate for the next day's racing.

I always stay at the Moat House Hotel for Doncaster. For the St Leger meeting it's usually full of racing people, trainers, breeders, owners, jockeys, who are all up for either the racing or the sales. Jack Berry is another regular and mentioned the fun of the place in his own book, *It's Tougher at the Bottom*. He always greets me with a reminder of a morning there: 'That Mr Thompson,' jokes Jack, 'a right show-off.' He's referring to the time when, staying as usual at the Moat House, I decided to take a sauna to freshen up. Jack was already having a sweat and asked me to get some water for the hot coals before I sat down. The only thing he didn't mention was that it was a mixed sauna, so when I walked out with nothing on to fill the sauna bucket from the shower there were more than a few embarrassed giggles.

In recent years the St Leger has come in for criticism over its format, and its demanding distance of one and three-quarter miles. Striking the right balance with the race can be difficult. The traditions must be respected – the St Leger distance is fiercely defended when it is suggested there should be a reduction – but there are the demands of the modern sporting and racing world to consider. Few races are run over such a trip. But it is always worth remembering how strongly people in Yorkshire feel about the St Leger when changes to the race are raised, be it the trip, or whether four-year-olds and older horses should be able to run in it, or whatever.

In the 1980s the prestige of the race certainly took a hammering when some winners had to beat only moderate fields to earn a Classic success. But I don't accept that this devalued the race: I don't subscribe to the theory that it's not the races you win, it's the horses you beat. In my mind, a Classic winner has to be a good horse. Some great fillies have won it without beating much, but they were great fillies: Oh So Sharp, User Friendly. Try telling George Duffield, brought up in Yorkshire's Malton, that User Friendly, whom he rode, wasn't a good horse. George is not someone you'd want to cut up in your car on the motorway. He calls a spade a spade. I think he might have something to say to anyone who suggested that User Friendly didn't beat anything with any ability when she won the St Leger in 1992.

The race should be the climax to the Triple Crown races. In 1970 Nijinsky completed the treble of the 2000 Guineas, the Epsom Derby and the St Leger but I fear this exceptional horse might have done the race more harm than good by winning it and completing the historic sequence. He was beaten in the Prix de l'Arc de Triomphe about a month later, and many believed the stamina demands of the St Leger trip cost him the race in Paris. From then on, three-year-olds with the aim of the Arc seemed to sidestep the St Leger. Nashwan is a prime example: he had the chance to complete the sweep in 1989 but missed the race to run in France in a trial for the Arc.

I suppose we have to accept – even those of us who love the St Leger – that today's horses are a different breed from those who were racing twenty-five years ago. The mile to ten-furlong horse is the horse of the nineties, with some horses staying the twelve furlongs of the Derby. The horses who excel at the St Leger distance of fourteen furlongs are the exception. But, that said, it was great that a true, quality stayer like Shantou won the race in 1996 with Frankie Dettori in the saddle. Great for the St Leger and great also for Shantou's trainer, John Gosden, who had been criticized in the *Sporting Life* during the summer for his record in the season's big races – rudely criticized in my opinion. Maybe it's the beginning of a revival in the race's fortunes. Whatever the future holds, I hope it's good for John. I always learn something when I talk to him. He puts across his views and then justifies them with sound argument. I wish all trainers would join the John Gosden School of Interviewees.

I'm home in the south at Newmarket for only a short time after the St Leger before the Channel 4 team returns north. This time we go even further, as far north as we go all season, to Ayr and the Western meeting. It will have been just a few days since Jack Berry was at the Doncaster sales and holding court and now he will have changed into Mr Ayr. He's great for racing everywhere in the north.

The Western meeting is three days of true Scottish hospitality, culminating in the Ayr Gold Cup on the Saturday, the last day of the fixture and Jack Berry's Derby. He loves it and has since he was a kid. Jack has a real feel for the Ayr crowd and for what owners, trainers and jockeys look for from the Western meeting. It was over a dinner with Mike Dillon, the excellent Ladbrokes racecourse representative, that Jack dreamed up the idea of an Ayr Silver Cup on the Friday for all the runners who are left out of the big one on Saturday because of the racecourse safety limit. What a great idea it was. I reckon they should have a Bronze Cup and even a Tin Cup. You'd get the runners.

Jack won the Ayr Gold Cup for the first time with So Careful in 1988. It was a dream come true for him, but I'm not sure that many people were on. The starting price was 33–1. The man to pick you a winner in the Ayr Gold Cup, or any sprint handicap for that matter, is my colleague on Channel 4, Alastair Down. He follows the form avidly. Mind you, picking the winner is no harder than commentating on this type of race: there are always big fields and everything happens in a flash. It's never easy.

I commentated on the Ayr Gold Cup in 1979, when Primula Boy won it by the narrowest of margins. Peter Bromley fell ill on the morning of the race and I had to fly up to Ayr at the last minute. I was booked into a hotel called the Savoy, which sounded great. Sadly, it was actually a big old house and I was in the smallest room at the top with one light-bulb and little else.

The Ayr meeting that year took place when ITV television was on strike, which added to the pressure of covering the race for radio: my commentary would be heard by as many as an extra million listeners. The finish was very tight and I wasn't sure who had won and called Valeriga, trained by Luca Cumani, as the winner. I think that Luca was actually getting married that day to Sara. They say he ordered some champagne on the strength of my verdict, which the judge reversed on sight of the photograph. I don't think Luca has forgiven me – yet.

But it isn't all hard work at Ayr. There's always some fun. There's an excellent Eve of Gold Cup press dinner – it's easy to tell who enjoyed themselves most the following day – and warm weather ensures a steady supply of ice-creams from a generous Scottish racing crowd. There are the usual pranks, too, which is a real Newmarket thing. Newmarket people – in fact, racing people – love to wind each other up. My sleep was interrupted at Ayr one year soon after I started working on television by a 4 a.m. alarm call. The culprits? Well, let's just say that Messrs Hodgson and Connorton from the weighing room were staying in the same hotel.

Scottish flat-racing people are a bit different from the jumping types, in the same way that Lambourn is a bit different from Newmarket. It's more town than country with a lot of Glaswegians making up the big turnout guaranteed for the Gold Cup. The Scottish tracks are full of character and offer racegoers some real contrasts. Racing holidays are popular, and at certain times of year you can enjoy unbroken periods of racing for a fortnight at places like Kelso, Hamilton, Perth and Edinburgh, now known as Musselburgh. In the days of travel allowances, when an owner was paid compensation by the Jockey Club for the costs incurred in the horse travelling a long distance to run, some trainers would take advantage of the clusters of fixtures in Scotland and send a horse up for three or four runs over a fortnight and claim the full allowance for a number of trips. It all helps.

Hamilton is a great Scottish track. Peter Savill, one of the richest men in racing, has a box there – a long way from his tax-haven home in the Cayman Islands! The track is superb. A few trainers, like Sir Mark Prescott, will travel up to Hamilton just for the ground. The great thing is, though, there's never any resentment if a Newmarket trainer has sent up a decent horse to race against weaker opposition. That is, as long as the trainer is a regular at Hamilton – as Sir Mark is – and supports the track. It's also nice to see local trainers like Linda Perratt and Peter Monteith. The Scots love a local winner.

In my days as a stable lad, Ken Oliver was the king of Scottish racing. With Barry Brogan up, a horse trained by Ken seemed invincible. They called him Benign Bishop. Great name. Of course, Ken was as invincible on the flat as he was over jumps. When he rode as an amateur he was a pretty good jockey, too. He told me once that an owner, who couldn't give him cash for his services in the saddle, promised him the 'best present a jockey's ever had' if he won a race. Weeks after Ken had obliged, he received a letter in the post from Muirfield Golf Club telling him that his application to join had been accepted. Membership of a course that had been known to turn away Open champions! The owner wasn't far wrong.

Ken was also instrumental in starting up Doncaster Bloodstock, along with Willie Stephens. The company is based in Hawick, which is more famous for knitwear and rugby union. It's strange that this small Scottish town is home to a thriving bloodstock concern with the Beeby family – one of Scotland's most famous racing families – still at the forefront.

My own memories of when my family had runners in Scotland are less triumphant. One year we had one with a chance at Kelso and Howard, my brother, was due to ride. These trips away together were always fun, but this time the Temperance Hotel we stayed in was, as its name suggests, something of a disappointment. Great on the sandwiches, not so good on the beer. Things didn't go much better at the races either. Howard fell at the first and the bridle came off, which meant I spent three hours catching the horse and more hours coaxing him back to the racecourse stables.

Things have changed since those days. I haven't been back to the Temperance Hotel for quite a few years. Instead, with all due respect to the management there, since that stay I've been lucky enough always to encounter good old-fashioned hospitality with drink when I venture north of the border – or, indeed, anywhere in the north – especially every September.

OCTOBER

Home and Away

In Newmarket October is like harvest time for all the local jockeys, trainers, owners, breeders, auctioneers and bloodstock agents – even the broadcasters. It's the yearling sales, auctioning the stars of tomorrow, which gives the town this great feel. They're in full swing in October and you can hear the sounds all over town of horses being bought and sold at the Tattersalls sales complex. If I open my windows and the wind is in the right direction I can just hear the auctioneer's voice. There is also, of course, top-quality racing throughout the month to coincide with the sales, back at the Rowley Mile after a summer at the July Course. This adds to the excitement. All the hotels are full of prospective owners, racegoers and journalists for some of Newmarket's most intriguing racing. It's a busy time for everyone who lives in the headquarters of English racing and the surrounding villages.

I sometimes like to go up to the Tattersalls sales ring, where some of the best racehorses of all time have been auctioned, and watch the bidding. It's amazing to see people spend so much money on horses in such a short space of time. It's frightening to hear the speed at which the amounts bid rise until the hammer falls. An electronic board hangs above the auctioneer's head which converts bids in guineas into all the currencies of the bloodstock world. The only denomination missing is dirhams, used in the United Arab Emirates and Dubai, which seems like an oversight, these days. After all, the Arabs have been known to buy the odd yearling or two. The sheikhs have their own room at Tattersalls where they decide whether they are going to bid on any of the prized lots and how much they are prepared to pay for a horse before it enters the ring.

I learn a bit from attending the auctions, too. Listening to the auctioneers can help me with my commentaries. The person on the rostrum trying to sell the horse for as much as he can has to strike a balance between cheekiness, bullying and reticence. So do I when I'm at the racecourse commentating. And what an auctioneer says about a horse helps me to decide when to take a pull and when to give it everything the next time I'm calling a finish. The Beebys are great value in coaxing out one last bid at Doncaster sales. At Tattersalls, Edward Mahony gives the impression of a bank clerk, but with a gavel in his hand he's a different man. You rarely catch him so talkative away from the rostrum.

I have bought a number of horses over the years, but despite what people think, we don't earn millions for working in television so I haven't nearly enough money for a string of racehorses in my name. A few years back I had a half share in a good sprinter called Music Machine, who won three races, which was great, and won three more after we had sold him, which still bothers me! A horse called Lion Tower, formerly trained by Henry Cecil and bred by Sheikh Mohammed, has raced for Julie and me in Dubai, thanks to Ahmed Al Shafar, one of Paddy Rudkin's owners. Ahmed, who has also had horses with John Dunlop and Robert Armstrong in England, bought us a colt in Dubai which we felt might win the showing class at the Horse of the Year Show. We saw this beautiful animal and talked about his potential so Ahmed, whose kitchen is bigger than the whole of my flat, stepped in and bought it from Ziad Galadari. The plan was to ship the horse to Britain, but sadly he died from complications after an operation to geld him. Julie was terribly upset. But within ten minutes of hearing this sad news, Ahmed was on the telephone to say that he had bought Lion Tower as a replacement. Owning a horse in Dubai is great value and much cheaper than the cost of having a horse in training in Britain, and the Dubai sales are developing slowly, too.

Newmarket's racing in October is a great mix. There are the high-quality races like the Champion Stakes, the Dewhurst, the Cheveley Park and Middle Park at the beginning of the month, and also the great handicaps, the Cesarewitch and the Cambridgeshire, which make up the bookmakers' autumn double. Newmarket plans to stage a day of Champions, which would usually fall on the month's last racing Saturday and feature the Champion Stakes and the Dewhurst. This would be a break from the past, but I reckon it would be a great day's racing. Great television, too.

You don't have to stage a Pattern race to attract good horses to run at Newmarket. The racing in October is sprinkled with Newmarket maidens, packed with horses full of promise for next season. There's plenty of gossip before a maiden, which adds to the feeling of anticipation that you might see a really good horse make a stunning début. I usually narrow a maiden field down to two or three Newmarket-trained runners if I'm advising punters on what to back, but I always remember that there may be something running from out of town – from Cole's or Dunlop's yard – to top the best of the home defence. The bookmakers' tissue – their early predictions of prices for later in the afternoon – is usually a good indication of which trainers have a good horse running. I also hear a lot of gossip when I get to the track – maybe a horse you haven't considered has been going well on the gallops – and late pointers make tipping pretty treacherous. Instead I try to pass on as much information as I've gathered before the race and leave the final decision in the hands of the punter.

Like tipping a maiden winner, commentating at Newmarket is especially tough. The Rowley Mile, which is just a long straight, isn't designed to make the lives of commentators easy. What's more, the race-course layout, with the starts to some races out of sight of the grandstand, means that the commentator is even more important to the crowd. Without him, racegoers who cannot see a television screen may not know what's happening until half the race is over, so the pressure is on to deliver an accurate picture of the horses in running. Commentators have to use a tele-vision monitor for races that are more than a mile and a half and it helps if it's a colour set. I remember one year finding that my picture for the Cesarewitch, which starts out of sight more than a mile from the grandstand and always attracts a huge field, was only in black and white.

In fact, autumn afternoons can present problems for commentators that the public may struggle to appreci-ate. Daylight hours finish earlier and earlier, which sometimes forces racecourses to cut things fine with the timing of the last race in relation to dusk. Believe me, when the sun is setting behind the stalls at, say, Leicester before the start of a twenty-runner maiden, it can be difficult enough to pick out the winner, let alone the fast-finishing third who might go on to make up into a Derby horse in less than a year's time. Peter Bromley's advice to me was always to try to pick out the winner with two furlongs to go and you'll be right seven times out of ten. I haven't done my fellow commentators any favours with the Thompson family's racing colours of light blue jacket with a yellow sash and sleeves and a white cap. Not easy to pick out with the sun in your eyes. Up to now, though, I haven't had to call Lion Tower home.

These are shared problems and there's a great rapport between racecourse commentators and broadcasters, which helps. The BBC's National Hunt pundit, Richard Pitman, and I always like to have a joke if we're sharing a Racing Channel broadcast, with him in the studio and me on the course. Richard once remarked on a red jacket I was wearing. I said it matched his eyes! Raleigh Gilbert is another who's great company, very supportive and with whom there's always the chance of some fun. Raleigh, who sometimes does Channel 4 commentary, is the man who still pulls out the white fivers. A few years ago, Mac and I once pretended we were receiving £800 each for a day's work at Tyne Tees, which was considerably more than the real fee. Raleigh, who was part of the team, was furious until he realized the wind-up. Legend also has it that he had to call for assistance from the Edinburgh fire brigade over the public address system at Musselburgh. He had got stuck in the commentary box, which has to be one of the smallest and most uncomfortable in Britain. I'm sure there have been times when he would have been happy to see Mac and me abandoned up there.

Away from home and Newmarket, one of the highlights for me in October is the Redcar Two-Year-Old Trophy. It was, of course, my home track for a long

time before Newmarket assumed the role. I loved
going to Redcar. Still do. They had the first colour
screen test from Redcar races in the 1950s. It didn't go
out on air, but there was a television in a tent on the
course where you could see the picture. I remember. I
was there. It makes me feel dead chuffed today to
think that the colour images viewers now enjoy and
take for granted all started from a test at Redcar, where
it all started for me too.

In the days of the ITV Seven, I worked at Redcar
quite often. It's a seaside course with the established
autumn highlight of the Zetland Gold Cup, now
rivalled in popularity by the Two-Year-Old Trophy
and its big prize. When I heard that the racecourse was
planning a new valuable two-year-old race in October
I had my reservations. I wasn't sure if there was room
in the racing calendar for another race for juveniles at
that stage in the season. It comes very late in the year
and there are plenty of other options around then for
any trainer with a good horse. But it seems to work
and has rapidly developed quite a following with its
innovative format. It's a great end-of-season target for
a small trainer with a good horse. The race rewards
smaller yards as on top of the purse there is a bonus for
the winning trainer and his or her stable, and the fewer
two-year-olds the trainer has registered with them, the
larger it is. This meant that in 1993 Alf Smith was really
in the money when he won it with Cape Merino. He
told me that he had only about three juveniles at the
time.

Channel 4 usually covers Redcar as part of a double-
header programme, covering racing from two meetings. Double-header meetings are quite tough from the
broadcasting point of view. It's up to nine races sometimes, which means it's bang, bang, bang, race, race,
race, without a break. That puts everyone on edge.

One thing is crucial: the two presenters needed for a successful double-header must be linked with sound. This may not seem essential but, believe me, it is. There has to be some exchange between the two presenters and if one says to the other in handing over, 'What's the racecourse mood like where you are?', there should be an appropriate response, otherwise the programme becomes disjointed. It is also important that the producers and directors can communicate with both courses. In fact, communication is the key to a successful double-header.

I learned the lesson of communication the hard way one Saturday when we were covering racing from Newmarket and France, a double-header featuring the Cambridgeshire and the card from Longchamp the day before the Prix de l'Arc de Triomphe. This was in the days when Channel 4 had the contract to cover the Arc. We had Graham Goode in Paris, along with Brough Scott, and Raleigh Gilbert in Newmarket, where I was fronting the British half of the programme. The problems began when I tried to hand over to GG at Longchamp as the runners went into the stalls for the start of the Prix du Cadran, a Group One stayers' test. There was nothing from Paris. No sound. Not a squeak. Andrew Franklin asked me through my earpiece to commentate for GG. At this point the infamous Newmarket wind got to grips with my *Sporting Life* and blew away some pages, which left me with no racecards for help. It was lucky that Sheikh Mohammed had two horses in the race carrying his familiar maroon and white silks and that one of his runners was a grey. English-based jockeys, with styles familiar to me, had taken the bulk of the rides, which also helped, and ultimately I muddled through, but I was near collapse at the end of the programme. Never again, if I can help it.

I miss not covering the Arc weekend in particular and French racing in general. The BBC won the contract back, which meant they were able to screen live Lammtarra's great win in the Prix de l'Arc de Triomphe in 1995. It was particularly sad to lose the French rights as over the years that we had the contract we had tried to build up the coverage. We took Channel 4 to Paris and did a full programme from Longchamp. We also covered the trials and racing throughout the season, from Chantilly and Deauville too.

I was disappointed because I have such fond memories of working in France as a young man. You'll remember me mentioning earlier that I was a pupil assistant for six months at Chantilly and those days were good ones. My time with Pierre Sanoner was full of experiences, and while I was there so were Pip Payne and Garde Grissell, now trainers in their own right. Michael Kauntze, too, was around a lot. He was assistant to Vincent O'Brien, who had plenty of French runners, and was a regular visitor. I always call him Micko, which he hates. He took out a licence to train in his own right and retired in 1996. Goodness, that makes me feel old!

As with all pupil assistants, I learned a lot about gardening. Monsieur Sanoner loved the stable's showpiece lawn, which was in the middle of the yard, but I only understood exactly how much after one of his string – a real pig of a horse – broke out of his box. I always rode this beast because I was the heaviest in the yard, which calmed him a bit. One day after morning exercise, I took off his bridle to let him have a roll in his box and he got out. He tried to mount everything, mares, fillies, colts, geldings, before taking a particular liking to the guv'nor's hallowed ground. It took me two days to replace the divots.

One year I went back to the old yard. I was in Paris before Channel 4's Arc weekend programme to interview the Aga Khan, whom I had got to know during the eighties from almost annual chats at Epsom on Derby Day. On arriving in Chantilly at the old Sanoner yard, the memories flooded back: no hot water, cramped accommodation, witches' brooms with no heads, a guv'nor of the old school who liked to go hunting after the first lot of horses had exercised. Sometimes when I drive past Pip Payne's Newmarket stables, I think that maybe if things had worked out differently I would be the one training and Pip and Garde could be working in television. Now there's a thought.

For the Channel 4 programmes from Paris, a skeleton team would go over for the Saturday, with those working at Newmarket – which always seemed to clash with the Saturday card at Longchamp – following after racing. We were a small part of a mini-invasion of largely British radio and television, which was usually in reverse as soon as racing was over on the Sunday. Great fun.

I have covered two Arcs, including Suave Dancer's great win in 1991, for NBC, the American television network. I worked as a presenter with the great Tom Hammond. For NBC, interviews had to be no more than forty-five seconds to fit in with the network television requirements, which was quite a contrast to the lengths I was used to for Channel 4. I had to wear a blazer, too, as part of the NBC sport presenter's uniform. You wouldn't believe it but these blazers are crucial to the programme. The station undertakes audience research to find out which colour is most comfortable on the viewer's eye. Incidentally, the NBC badges are stick-on Velcro.

Tom Durkin, the race-caller for NBC who did the

commentary on the Arc, became a good friend. I once told him I loved the way he always included in his commentaries the phrase 'and down the stretch they come'. Tom was touched by the flattery. Then he said, 'Thank you, Derek, but it's not me who says that.' A good friend and a forgiving one, I hope!

It was great the year that Suave Dancer won. Cash Asmussen, for whom I had acted as an agent in the past, rode the winner, who was bred by his father. After the race, which the horse won brilliantly, Cash, in his own unique way, turned to the camera and said, 'I won this for the US of A.' Perfect.

Inevitably, some of the other Arc day interviews I have attempted – like some others I've already mentioned – didn't go quite so well. Yves Saint Martin only speaks English when he wants to. Although my O-level French improved in leaps and bounds during six months in Chantilly, it wasn't good enough to persuade the great man that because I was making the effort he should open up in English. The late François Boutin, one of the greatest French trainers of all time, was another who would not speak English on air. His wife, Lucy Respoli, acted as interpreter. Thierry Jarnet, one of André Fabre's jockeys, is another story altogether. He doesn't speak English very well and, in fact, can't really do interviews. It was easier to understand his reluctance when one day at Newmarket this was explained to me!

It would be great if my French was better but I did turn this limitation to my advantage once on air. It was when I hosted the worldwide phone-in before the first Dubai World Cup. Early on in the broadcast a French caller went on about some point for two minutes. The panel, which included Brough Scott and Clive Brittain, all looked puzzled so I thanked the caller – *merci* – for his interest and then asked the gathered experts whether they could explain why there was no French horse in the inaugural running of the richest race in the world. This was, shall we say, a fairly loose translation of the original! Ignorance is sometimes bliss.

From a professional point of view – and putting to one side my personal disappointment – I feel that the BBC decided to win back the coverage of the Arc at least partly because we on Channel 4 had done so much to build it up and increase the popularity of French racing on Britain. Losing an event is a real blow. It's a pity that all stations can't have access to events and leave the viewer to make up his or her own mind which coverage they prefer. But, in today's world of media rights, deals are done and trades are made. Many of my colleagues were upset to lose Paris but, then, we took Cheltenham from the BBC. It's swings and roundabouts. At least, though, the Prix de l'Arc de Triomphe is shown live on British television. All in all, October is a great month for television viewers. There are plenty of domestic double-headers mixed in with coverage of the main races from all over Europe and the world. Channel 4 and the BBC together offer a great blend, looking forward to next year as well as bringing to your home the autumn's high points.

In television, we take a lot of criticism in October – and every other month, for that matter. But it is especially hard to understand in this month, bearing in mind what is on offer to the public. I've mentioned the letters to the *Sporting Life* and *Racing Post* that followed the interview with Henry Cecil after Bosra Sham had won the Champion Stakes. But viewers must try to understand that to make the programmes better we have to take a few chances – to experiment. This means, inevitably, that it doesn't always work. For example, after In Command had won the Dewhurst

Stakes, I interviewed Michael Hills, the colt's jockey, as he walked back to the weighing room. It was very spontaneous – 'Hey, Derek, that was brilliant, top of the day' – and a great bit of television, catching a jockey's excitement immediately after he has won a big race. The only problem was that Biffo, my camera-man who was walking backwards filming, tripped and crashed to the floor with the camera still on his shoulder. I was still on screen and had to keep address-ing the camera and Michael couldn't help him – he hadn't weighed in. I couldn't abandon the programme and Michael wasn't about to forfeit a Group One win-ner by being disqualified, so neither of us could help Biffo. 'Is he all right?' Michael asked me. He was. Poor Biffo! A good idea that didn't quite come off.

I find letters critical of me to the racing papers from the public quite hurtful. Brough Scott, who is editorial director of the *Racing Post*, encourages me to write in and defend myself, but I don't think it's the right thing to do.

A lot of people say racing journalists and television commentators are a tame bunch. I suppose it's true, to a certain extent, but we all have to live together. Even so, there are jockeys, trainers and owners – we all know who they are – who will give interviews either only to the BBC or only to Channel 4. They seem to miss the point that we have two hundred days' racing on television a year – for free. We should all support it. More television means more sponsorship and general exposure, which can only be good for the game.

There's no point in holding grudges for too long. Or getting too steamed up about racing on television. Sometimes the whole thing has to be put into perspec-tive. In 1987, when the terrible storms caused devasta-tion nationwide I was living in the north. It was Newmarket's two-day Champion Stakes meeting and

I stayed in Cambridge on the Thursday before Friday's Dewhurst and the Channel 4 programme. On the night of the storms it was pretty windy. When I woke at 7 a.m. I listened to the news, and decided to drive over to Newmarket – usually a twenty-minute journey – to see for myself how bad things were. It took me over two hours to get there. As racing was abandoned – the track was probably fine but there was no way the horses could have made the journey – we did a feature on the chaos that had resulted from the high winds. We filmed up the Bury Road where nine out of ten trees – some mighty oaks that had been there for decades – had fallen. Every ten yards, it seemed, a magnificent tree was lying on the ground. It was like the Blitz, but this time with trees, not buildings. It took a month to clear the mess. The sight of those great oaks reminded me that racing isn't everything.

The clash in 1996 of the Cheveley Park day at Newmarket with the Labour Party conference also put racing in context. It was an important political occasion as it was the last round of conferences before the general election and we had to give way. We started our programme at the usual time, then Channel 4 cut to the conference half-way through. We recorded the racing to show when we resumed broadcasting after the keynote speeches of the afternoon. There's a world going on outside racing and this was a good reminder to me of our place in the grand scheme of things.

The next person who complains about Channel 4's racing coverage should talk to anyone who watched that day's interrupted broadcast on a television set in Dubai. There, the racing was screened throughout the afternoon, uninterrupted, with the Channel 4 team, in all its glory, scratching noses and chatting away to each other in relaxed off-camera mood, unaware that what we thought was off-air footage was going out live in Dubai. An afternoon of that would be enough to convince anyone that Channel 4 in particular and television coverage in general in Britain is actually not half bad.

NOVEMBER

Changing Seasons

At the beginning of November, Julie teases me that I slip on a black armband to mark the passing of another flat season as some of the thoroughbred stars of Newmarket, Epsom, Ascot, York, Goodwood and Doncaster retire to stud, and Frankie and Co. move from centre stage. It's not entirely fair. I admit I probably prefer summer racing and the glamour of the flat, but in November, I'm excited at the prospect of a fresh start to the jumps. After Cheltenham in March, top-quality jumps racing begins to wind down with just the Grand National and the Whitbread at Sandown to come. Then I think, that's the end of the quality jumping for a year, so now let's get ready for the new flat season.

It's the same for any sports fan who follows, say, cricket and football. They might also have a favourite but when one season ends they start looking forward to the climaxes of the other sport ahead. In spring, after the Cup Final at Wembley, they start to look forward to Test matches, one-day internationals and finals at Lords. In September, it's the thought of the Cup Final again and league title deciders that excites. In

[145]

November, I'm looking forward to Kempton on Boxing Day, jumping at Sandown and, of course, Cheltenham in March. I love it – *almost* as much as flat racing.

I'm not one to begrudge flat trainers a good long holiday in the Barbados sun, either. Why shouldn't they enjoy a decent break in the winter? They can't go at any other time of year. In fact, not many of them go to 'Newmarket-on-Sea', these days. At least, not as many as used to. Today trainers are as likely to go to Dubai, which is expanding rapidly as a leisure destination. It's relaxing, even if you find yourself on the beach next to Ben Hanbury and his busy mobile phone.

It's worth remembering too, before people start criticizing, that many of the top trainers work virtually the whole year round. The expanding international racing calendar sees to that. Races like the Arlington Million signal the beginning of the transatlantic autumn – or fall – competition season as early as August. The Washington International keeps it on the boil, and the Breeders' Cup in November is its climax. The best trainers also look east to the Japan Cup and down-under to Australia and the Melbourne Cup. Top trainers work hard, no doubt about that.

The Godolphin team is now at the forefront of world racing. They are seeking winning opportunities all over the globe. Geographically, Dubai is perfectly placed to look west, east, and even south for races to win and to take advantage of the expanding world racing calendar. The Dubai operation's ambitions are mirrored by other pioneering trainers from Europe who want to win races everywhere for the owners of their own stable stars, trainers like Clive Brittain, Dermot Weld, Michael Stoute, Henry Cecil, John Gosden, André Fabre. Our best jockeys, Frankie

Dettori, Pat Eddery, and Walter Swinburn, want to be world stars, too. And don't forget Johnny Murtagh, Breeders' Cup Mile hero on Ridgewood Pearl.

The Breeders' Cup in November is the real challenge. What a great idea it was that the Kentucky horseman John Gaines came up with nearly twenty years ago. His theory was that if breeders could be persuaded to part with a registration fee for each of their foals to make them eligible to run in future prestigious races as two-year-olds, and at three, four and older, a huge pool of dollars would be established to fund the races. Gaines was right. So simple. Breeders have to register because they don't want to deny the foal the chance to run if it turns out to be good enough and so many foals are bred every year in America that huge funds are generated by the registration scheme. Enough to support a host of races carrying massive prizes and staged on a single championship day: the Breeders' Cup as we know it today.

I don't think there's room in the European calendar for our own Euro Breeders' Cup, but that doesn't mean that the American concept is in any way diminished and its races any less worth winning. British-based trainers should always look at the Breeders' Cup as the pinnacle of a flat horse's career. Newmarket's innovative day of Champions, incorporating the Dewhurst and Champion Stakes, is one thing, but we should still single out the Breeders' Cup races of this month as a target for our best horses. Winning a Breeders' Cup race at the end of a hard season is almost the ultimate a European or Dubai-based horse can achieve.

Peter Amos is moving with the times here and does everything he can to help trainers prepare for the different challenge of winning races on dirt surfaces and round unfamiliar tracks. The all-weather tracks help, too, by letting trainers work contenders on the

Equitrack and Fibresand if they think it will help prepare horses for a Breeders' Cup race. We should all follow Peter's example – and that of the all-weather
venues – and support the effort to win Breeders' Cup
races with European-trained horses. Beating the
Americans in their own backyard gives British racing
a big boost.

It's not only jockeys and trainers who find themselves doing extra air miles at the end of the year on the
back of the expanding international racing calendar.
I've done a few Breeders' Cups on location in America
for Channel 4. In 1991 I was privileged to be at
Churchill Downs for Arazi's win in the Breeders' Cup
Juvenile for colts. I remember someone asking me
what I thought about the horse's chances before the
race. I said I thought he'd win. It was then that the
stranger told me that he owned a runner in the same
race as Arazi, that his horse was a speed horse and
when he heard the bell that sounds when the runners
break from the starting stalls, it would be whoosh! he's
gone. After watching Arazi and the way he wove
through the field on the far 'back stretch' side of the
course, the owner was speechless. So were most
people. I nearly was, too.

Julie gets the old Union Jack flags out for Breeders'
Cups when I'm at home in Newmarket for the
evening, UK time, and the races are being screened,
afternoon time, in America. There's a real buzz in the
town, which looks forward to the night and the challenge it presents to our best horses, jockeys and trainers. In 1996 we had a party for the Breeders' Cup,
which was staged for the first time at Woodbine in
Canada. It was an emotional meeting. Walter
Swinburn rode Pilsudski for the Weinstocks and
Michael Stoute, and there were plenty of tears when he
won the Breeders' Cup Turf. Remember that Walter

had suffered a horrific fall at the beginning of the year in Hong Kong that nearly cost him his life. He had spent six months out of the saddle, waiting for the Jockey Club to give him back his licence. He was also ending a long Breeders' Cup losing run for his boss, Michael, and won the race for the Weinstock family which had suffered the loss of Simon, a great racing enthusiast, to cancer. That night, Cigar, the great American champion racehorse, was beaten on his final outing in the Breeders' Cup Classic, after his jockey Jerry Bailey, had ridden a less than brilliant race. As Jerry had been critical in the past of Walter and some other European jockeys going round America's tight dirt tracks in Breeders' Cup races, it was a great chance for Walter to even the score and no second invitation was needed. 'Frankie would have won by two lengths if he had been riding Cigar,' said Walter, the hero of the day. But it was because Walter was back in the big time that made it so special for me.

I have flown to quite a few race meetings with Walter, who has his own plane to ease the travel burden. My two sons, Alex and James, know it on sight in the sky and always point it out as it flies overhead. I was pleased to have been the racecourse commentator at Windsor in July 1996 when he rode a winner on his comeback ride after his recovery. Walter started 1997 in great spirits but took a sabbatical shortly after the start of the season. His weight was a problem – Walter is quite broad for a jockey – and I think he needed time away from race riding to allow his metabolism to settle down after such a tough year.

I have worked with Walter on Channel 4 a few times now. He helped out during his recuperation from the Hong Kong fall – we sneaked him from under the noses of the BBC for the meeting. They had asked him to work at the Greenham meeting at Newbury so we booked him for the Craven meeting at Newmarket a few days before. As a result, the BBC dropped him. They rang back two weeks later to try to book him again for another meeting, but Walter said he was too busy preparing for his next Channel 4 broadcast!

Now Sky has taken over the rights to the Breeders' Cup. Channel 4 cannot expect to cover the event live as the racing takes place in the afternoon in America and Saturday evening is too popular a slot on the Channel 4 schedule for racing to secure air time. In this respect racing struggles in America, too, perhaps even more so than it does in Britain. In the USA, it isn't as easy to have a bet as it is in Britain, and as about nine out of ten people watch racing so that they can have a punt on it, this limits the potential audience.

On Breeders' Cup day, at Channel 4 we have to make do with a telephone link-up before racing gets under way on the other side of the Atlantic, with a trainer or jockey at the meeting. At Woodbine in 1996, it was Henry Cecil who joined us on our afternoon broadcast from Doncaster. At the time, he was locked in a battle for the trainer's title with Godolphin's Saeed Bin Suroor, which he virtually forfeited that very afternoon when Medaaly scored for Godolphin in the Racing Post Trophy at Doncaster, picking up a big purse. We spoke to Henry after the race, as well as before, and he was very gracious in defeat.

Recently, racecourses like Doncaster, Ascot and Windsor have hosted Breeders' Cup dinners, screening the Sky coverage for guests. At some I've enjoyed working as master of ceremonies. In 1993, I was at Uttoxeter with the track's owner, Stan Clarke, and his wife, Hilda. I wasn't sure if the racecourse, which is not exactly at the centre of the flat-racing world, would attract a Breeders' Cup audience and my fears were partly confirmed when a local member who farms near the racecourse asked why there was no grass and no fences for the racing on the American course. That took a bit of explaining, but it was nothing to the problems I faced when Hilda fainted! She had been sitting next to me and we had been pooling bets all night right up until the last, the Breeders' Cup Classic. It was at this point that she complained of feeling light-headed and before anyone could get her a glass of water she fell back in her chair. I thought, I know I'm boring, but not *that* boring. The panic was over quickly, thanks to an American dentist, who was also a fully trained medic. However, a greater moral crisis developed for me while Hilda was recovering: Arcangues, my – or should I say our joint? – selection for the Breeders' Cup Classic, romped home in the race at odds of about 150–1. Of course, having fainted, Hilda did not know who our selection was so I was faced with the dilemma after the race when she'd recovered of either confessing and paying her half the money – more than £1000 – or keeping quiet and saying we'd backed yet another loser on my recommendation. I offered Mrs Clarke her share in the hope that she might say I could keep the lot for being so honest. I hadn't bargained for the wife of Uttoxeter racecourse's owner having her husband's keen sense of commercial opportunity. A Clarke – Stan or Hilda – never misses a trick, and I had to pay up Hilda's half in full. Even so, a great night all round.

I've never been involved work-wise during November with a Japan Cup or a Melbourne Cup, other than to introduce a recording of the race as part of a Channel 4 afternoon programme. The time difference – up to eleven hours – means that we are even less likely to be able to broadcast these races live than the Breeders' Cup. And anyway, for now, with little foreign form printed in the newspapers, there isn't a huge interest in them, even with more and more

European-trained horses running, especially in Australia. Betting-shop punters have no involvement with the majority of jockeys riding as many are unfamiliar to them, apart from a handful of the biggest names from Europe who make the journey.

It might be that the timing of international racing around the world presents an opportunity for the Racing Channel. The former Corals man, George Irvine, fronts the new satellite station, which already seems to have secured a foothold with serious followers of racing since it began in 1995. If the Racing Channel ever goes twenty-four hours, like a lot of specialist satellite stations have, it might be able to justify screening events like the Melbourne Cup and the Japan Cup live for its highly committed audience. The audience the Racing Channel attracts is exactly the sort that would set the alarm clock for the 4 a.m. from Melbourne, especially if the Cup had a few European-trained runners with a real chance and some of our jocks riding them.

I might have ended up working on the Racing Channel as a studio presenter. I was asked and offered a decent contract and some good money, but after Andrew Franklin made it clear that I could not do it on top of the work that I am contracted to do for Channel 4, I had to turn the chance down. I slept on the offer I received – well, as much as you do in these circumstances – but Andrew's ruling meant it wasn't an option for me. Nevertheless, I fully support the Racing Channel. It's a great potential nursery for young commentators, is great for racecourses in helping them attract extra sponsorship, and the pictures from SIS are quite cheap. It is a pleasure to be involved to the degree that I am: as a commentator, along with all the other SIS contracted microphones, reporting before and after racing as well as covering the day's events on the track, live for the channel's committed audience. Let's hope it goes on to even better things.

So much for racing abroad during November. Back at home, the scheduling of the end of the flat season does its best to disguise that the big boys have largely finished for the year domestically and that it's only the all-weather and a chance for some of the smaller stables until March. Recently the turf season's final fixture has been at Folkestone on the Monday after Doncaster on Saturday, and frankly, with all due respect to the racecourse and its management team, it's a bit like, as the Americans say, kissing your sister. A non-event. I'm glad that 1997 got it right by drawing the curtain at Donny on Saturday with its final flat race meeting of the year.

The flat season always used to end at Doncaster on Saturday. Everything rounded off with the November Handicap, which we televised on Channel 4. The race is a good betting heat, there's always a massive crowd to see the champion trainer and jockey receive trophies for their efforts during the year and the season finished on a high instead of a whimper. To be fair, if you'd been at Folkestone in 1995 for the season's final day on Monday, you would have seen a Royal Ascot winner in the making – Pivotal – but, even so, you can't have the season fizzling out like that on the first day of the week without any television coverage. Apparently, the reason behind the Monday finish was that the authorities wanted to extend the flat season a full week after Doncaster into what has been traditionally the 'Mackeson weekend' at Cheltenham, but only Folkestone wanted a fixture in the week after Doncaster's Saturday finale. But why not just keep the final day at Donny and leave it at that?

I suppose you could make the same criticism of the jumps season which, with the introduction of summer jumping a few years ago, doesn't really have an end any more, or a beginning for that matter. I'm not really in favour of summer jumping. I just don't see the point of it. Sometimes the ground is rock-hard. After all, jumps racing goes on for ten months of the year already. Anyway, almost regardless of what has gone on before from June to October, I think for nearly everyone – punters certainly – November's Mackeson weekend signals the unofficial start of the jumps season proper. It's Cheltenham's first really important meeting and that sends out the message that jumping is again the number-one game in play until March.

Before the Mackeson, or what is now known as the Murphys Gold Cup, Channel 4 has usually done a few double-header broadcasts, which bring together the two codes from the likes of Wetherby and Newmarket. It certainly stirs my blood a bit when I'm standing in the Rowley Mile paddock and there's a great finish to a big chase up north to watch on the monitor. But it's not until November and the Murphys that jumps racing really grabs my attention. November comes and you think 'jumping' straight away. You don't do that in October, even for Wetherby's Charlie Hall Memorial Chase, which often attracts a quality, if select, field to Yorkshire.

The Murphys is a great curtain raiser to the season, unofficial or otherwise. Over a trip of two and a half miles, it's jumping at speed and is a great occasion with which to kick off the season proper for our television audience. Good horses will always come out for the Murphys, horses with the speed to lie up off the pace and the stamina to manage the last half-mile up that tough Cheltenham hill. It's great that Channel 4 has added Cheltenham to its schedule. And when the Murphys produces a good finish – which it usually does – I already know exactly how I'll wind up the programme when we clock off: 'If we have more finishes like that this year, we're in for a great jumps season.'

The last running of the Mackeson, in 1995, before its name change, was as the middle Saturday feature race of a three-day Friday to Sunday meeting. It was the first fully fledged Sunday affair from the home of National Hunt racing to be televised on Channel 4. As you know I'm not the biggest fan of Sunday racing but I remember Brough's comment: 'Ours not to reason why. We're just the ones who put on the show for the viewers.' I sometimes wish he wasn't so easy-going about it!

From here on, after the Murphys, the action follows thick and fast in the jumps racing calendar – often seven days a week. The good horses are seen out more than their flat counterparts. Two weeks later, the Hennessy Cognac Gold Cup at Newbury is upon us. I'm going to have to wait to cover this race for tele-vision as it's very much part of the BBC's schedule, but it's still one of the top ten jumps races in the world for me. For the speed horses, there's the Mackeson. For the staying chaser, there's the Hennessy. The soft ground at Newbury around this time can make it a real test of stamina, but the course is fair and suits a good staying chaser. The old battlers can peak for this race as part of an autumn campaign before going on to Kempton and the King George VI, enjoy a break in January and come back for the Cheltenham Festival in March.

The Hennessy, and Whitbread's support of Sandown in April and the first big Cheltenham meet-ing of the year featuring the Murphys, are examples of long-term sponsorship deals in which the race is named after a company or its product, which over the years becomes part of racing's vocabulary. In 1996 Whitbread plc ended the Mackeson branding of its big occasion for commercial reasons and that year the race was run for the first time as the Murphys. Martin Pipe saddled the winner, Challenger Du Luc, and although a few purists may dispute this, I'm sure that the large prize was as valued as it would have been under any name. All in all, we're probably just lucky that Whitbread, with all the class you would expect of such a big, prestigious sponsor, supports racing. I know that races can end up running under some crazy names – the Mr Chris Cream Cakes Handicap, for example! – but really we can't complain about it. It's not our money so we have no say in what the sponsors want to call their event. Whitbread was the first company to sponsor races, so the Mackeson (or the Murphys or whatever the company wants to call the race) was always in safe hands. In fact, the name-change seemed to attract hardly any protest. In a few years, it will seem as if it has always been called the Murphys.

As for your own money, at this time of year – at least for a short while – I can tip both National Hunt and flat horses, which helps in maximizing the chance of me giving you a nice-priced winner. By mid-November, though, apart from occasionally selecting one for the all-weather from a Newmarket yard that keeps its horses on the go all year round, I'm selecting exclusively from National Hunt fields and I begin to nap jumpers full time. I usually choose the best bet of the day by looking at which yards are in form – Philip Hobbs and Martin Pipe early in the season, Jenny Pitman nearer this time of year, Gordon Richards almost any time – but the jumping form is there for everyone to see. Great horses put it in year after year. It's not like the flat where there are hidden talents and you have to listen to every whisper. Find a runner with previous form and see if the yard is firing.

I like to do all my tipping work, the phone lines and

the service on Teletext, in the morning. In the summer you never know what information you might pick up during an evening at, say, the Plough, and in winter, the going is so crucial and can easily change overnight. I make sure that the phone lines – an Irish one, the *Sporting Life* line, and Tommo's Newmarket Racing Club – are available by 8 a.m., update my Newmarket line two hours later and the *Sporting Life*'s service by midday. Just in case you think it's a scam, I don't get paid any extra for my insight if you call at a premium time, costing yourself a little extra in telephone charges. It's British Telecom that benefits from the higher call rate, not me.

The tipping lines mean some early starts, and in November the season of racing dinners has also begun to get under way, which adds to the struggle and setting up in the dark. The stable lads' boxing night in London is one such occasion when I sometimes wish that I worked alongside my old colleague from radio days, Desmond Lynam, on *Sportsnight*, without the crack-of-dawn work shifts that the racing world demands. I worked for nine years with 'Lyne', pronounced Line, his nickname, which everyone in radio sport used in his Radio 2 days. He's a smashing fellow with a lovely voice and attitude, who was always going to make it on television. Some years ago, Lyne, who loves his racing and has owned a share in the odd horse, came to the stable lads' night and joined us afterwards in the old racing watering hole, the Stork Club in Piccadilly, along with Champ, Colin Tinkler and Robin 'Bonzo' Barwell, who was assistant to Toby Balding before taking out his own licence to train in 1990.

Our bill that night was about £250 which in those days – the seventies – was a lot of money. As we left, the doorman reminded us that we had yet to settle the account and Lyne, who is not the most athletic of individuals – I have seen him almost bowl himself out LBW at cricket – knew that doing a runner was not an option, even though we had only about a fiver between us. Quick as a flash (certainly a lot quicker than he can run) Lyne nominated Bonzo, under the table at the time having accounted for the largest proportion of the bar bill, as in charge of clearing the debt.

Since then, Novembers have slowed down for me – and, I'm sure, for Des, too, even if his routine allows for the odd lie-in.

DECEMBER

All Weathers

If we make it to December without losing any racing to the cold weather, we've done pretty well. But the Christmas month is when blank days without any racing, except all-weather cards, become a distinct possibility. The frost stays in the ground, snow settles, and melted snow causes waterlogging. On any of these counts it's curtains for racing on the turf. On the days when there is racing, it's usually pretty cold. I start hearing in my earpiece pleadings from Andrew Franklin to try at least to 'look warm' even when it's freezing. In case you're still wondering, at the races I'm the one jogging on the spot next to a shivering bloke holding a camera. Out comes the camel coat – and it stays on for most of the next four chilly months ahead.

The bad weather of December can mean a lot of time and effort going to waste for everyone. I prepare as thoroughly in December as I do in any month of the year for commentating or a Channel 4 programme, even though I know that some of the work will never see the light of day. When racing is abandoned it's not like a day off sick from work or a holiday. For me, the rest of the Channel 4 team and all the trainers, jockeys, owners and racecourse staff who have been working towards the afternoon's card, it's a big disappointment. Unless the racing is abandoned early enough, say the day before, preparation has been going on and much of it is wasted. I've studied the form for the day's runners, planned most of the interviews and links, and written many of them too. After all this work, we want racing to go ahead as much as anyone.

Sometimes, quick thinking can save the day – and at least some of my preparation. If any racing that we can cover is unaffected by the weather, Channel 4 does its best to air it or, at least, save the abandoned meeting for another day's programme. Top races have been rescheduled or switched from track to track – like Ascot's Victor Chandler Chase which was run at Warwick one year – and sponsorship money saved, although sometimes moving a race can create a kerfuffle between ourselves and the BBC over broadcasting rights. The phone lines can be pretty busy in December between racecourses, Andrew Franklin, Mark Jackson (another key member of the Channel 4 executive team) and the British Horseracing Board.

Lingfield and its all-weather Equitrack came to the rescue in January 1997 when Channel 4's scheduled racing from Sandown Park was abandoned due to frost. The first Saturday of the new year opened therefore with the first all-weather card to top the bill on Channel 4 racing. It deserved its billing: that day showed that the all-weather scene deserves greater recognition than it usually receives – good betting contests, a good atmosphere, a fair crowd and an entertaining afternoon's racing. The viewing figures weren't bad either, considering that quite a few regulars must have planned a different Saturday afternoon from their usual Channel 4 routine when, in the middle of the week, the prospects for racing looked bleak.

I've been a fan of all-weather racing since day one, and not just because it has saved Channel 4's Saturday programme once or twice. Wolverhampton's big all-weather day in December I think shows the true potential of this type of racing for the future: it puts on something that makes the jumping tracks realize that they're in a competitive market for racegoers throughout the winter months. Look at it this way. The Americans have been hosting dirt racing for well over a hundred years and they manage to put on quite a show, don't they? There's nothing fundamentally wrong with racing on an artificial surface. So why not try to match the Americans with the racing at Wolverhampton, Lingfield and Southwell, Britain's three dirt tracks?

Wolverhampton stages a cracking December renewal of Britain's first listed race on the dirt, the Bass Wulfrun Stakes. The day may not rival the Kentucky Derby yet, but it is an emerging occasion which may grow into something big if a sponsor can put up a substantial purse – in 1996 it carried £50,000 in added money – to tempt owners and trainers. The likes of John Gosden, Mark Johnston, David Loder and Clive Brittain, as well as other top trainers, have all felt it worth their while to send runners. In 1996, there was even a Norwegian challenge to give the occasion a 'Euro-Breeders' Cup feel. What a great day it was. And one that can become even better if everyone supports it.

I love the way Ron Muddle, who owns Wolverhampton, has turned Saturday all-weather racing – especially the floodlit cards – into a real occasion. On a Saturday night, Wolverhampton boasts the busiest restaurant in racing. It may well be cold and wet outside, but the grandstand is nice and warm. Go and try it. You might even enjoy it! It really comes into its own in December. Remember that in 1963 there was no racing in Britain for three months because of the severe winter. Today, all-weather racing keeps the show on the road (and racing on Channel 4). Okay, even with Ron's efforts in staging a £50,000 race, which is good money by any standards, the best horses are still giving Wolverhampton a miss. But a 5–1 winner of a competitive contest is a 5–1 winner, even if the result won't be recorded in the history books of fifty years' time. Ron always takes the time and trouble to come up to the commentary box to say hello whenever I'm working there. And it's not only Wolverhampton racecourse that he's managed to turn round. He did a great job at Lingfield, too, when he owned that track. And at Southwell, which he also owns and which boasts its own golf course to boot.

For the jockeys, too – some of the lesser lights of the weighing room who spend the summer at secondary meetings away from the Ascots and the Epsoms – all-weather racing is a bonus. Jimmy Quinn, who took over a thousand rides in 1996, would never have reached such a milestone if it wasn't for the all-weather – nor would his driver have clocked up over seventy thousand miles in the season – and the extra rides can make a big difference to the finances of a struggling jockey who might have a young family to support. What they earn on the all-weather is reward for sheer hard work.

I'm not so sure about all-weather racing during the summer, though. Do we need it? It may mean an extra card to tip from but it certainly doesn't make picking winners for you any easier. Most of the all-weather horses boast some decent form of sorts on the dirt, which can make it hard to pick out a winner when they come up against each other in races. And some talented horses on the turf just don't make the transition to the dirt, which can lead to a few losing dirt-début selections based on available grass form. But what can you do? It's a brave tipster who ignores turf form when a horse is making its début on the all-weather. They're not all like Singspiel, as happy on the dirt as on the turf. It's one of the mysteries of racing, why good turf horses don't always go on the dirt, and vice versa. But the secret behind the success of Wolverhampton is less of a puzzle: like the jockeys who ride there, week in, week out, it's due reward for hard work.

December is a pretty tough month for me, too, certainly in terms of miles on the clock. The Dubai season is beginning to shape up and I have to fly out once or twice to do the commentary at Nad Al Sheba. I need Julian, my driver, quite a lot as I also find myself visiting some of the jump racing's smaller 'gaffs' tracks with the Racing Channel, SIS and for promotional commitments.

The competition for viewers between BBC and Channel 4 hots up this month, so on Channel 4 we have to be at our best. A lot of Saturdays have both BBC and Channel 4 racing in the afternoon – Chepstow and Sandown, Cheltenham and Haydock, Ascot and Uttoxeter often pair off in the December fixture list. Whatever the quality of racing, in my mind Channel 4 is at the day's number-one meeting – even when we're at what might be described as the day's 'secondary meeting'. But I never consider the racing we're showing to be second division. You have to think you're number one, whatever else is going on. After all, that's what the racegoers, jockeys, trainers and owners think. To help the viewer come to the same conclusion, and make the right choice for the bulk of the afternoon, the adverts are usually well timed, with an eye on the other channel's racing coverage. Don't be too surprised when a commercial break from Sandown coincides with the big race on the Beeb from Chepstow (during the summer, too!).

On the 'off-screen' days, when I'm not due to appear on Channel 4, there's sometimes the real treat of a December midweek visit to a small track for SIS or, as I said, to do some corporate entertainment work. Smaller tracks have a charm all of their own and the reception you get from the management and racegoers is great, compared with some of the bigger, more prestigious venues. The gaffs tracks seem to want to do more for racegoers *and* those of us who work in racing. For example, a top track like Newbury, for all its quality racing, has those terrible lifts, which are dreadful for anyone who is working or wants to look at the horses in the paddock, have a bet *and* get a good viewing spot for the race. I once nearly missed the start of a race on which I was commentating when the lift went from the ground to the fifth floor, where the commentary box is, and back down again without the doors opening. There were only two left to go into the stalls when I got there by the more dependable if exhausting stairs. I was gasping when I got to the mike. A close finish, even before the race.

We should be careful before we close any of Britain's smaller racecourses. For some racegoers, the gaffs venues are the only racecourses to which they can manage a visit. The local regulars at Sedgefield on a Tuesday may not be able to travel to York for another day of the week or afford the admission charges of the bigger tracks. Ludlow has no grandstand to speak of and Hexham is on the side of a hill, but the racecourse enclosures there are often full of people who want to have just the odd each-way punt and play the Placepot. Cartmel has the worst view of the racing in the country and attracts good crowds. These racegoers come to see good horses and quality runners at gaffs tracks more often than you might think. You see Cheltenham horses running at the gaffs. Mrs Pitman often saddles a good one at Plumpton.

And look at what Uttoxeter has achieved! It is a hugely popular racecourse that stages great racing despite not being a glamorous location. Maybe it's a bit more high profile than a gaffs track but it has made the best of what it has, through the great business brain of Stan Clarke and the sheer enthusiasm of the management and staff. Stan has been quick to take advantage of the publicity from the success he enjoyed in winning the Monday Grand National with Lord Gyllene. Uttoxeter was the horse's first port of call for a public appearance, and the track is going to name a race after him – just two examples of the management style that has helped Uttoxeter thrive. So has Newcastle, which has turned the corner since Stan took over. I'm a great supporter of these two racecourses and all the gaffs tracks. Always will be.

The real quality in December for me – and everyone – comes first at Cheltenham at the beginning of the month, and then, of course, at Kempton on Boxing Day. I've been going to the King George VI Chase there since 1972 for radio and television, and before that as an ordinary racegoer. I love it. There are people still coming into the car parks after racing has started and even after the big race itself. (I once saved Neale Doughty, then a young seven-pound claimer, from a similar fate when I saw a hitchhiker with saddle on the side of the M1 as I travelled down from Middlesbrough after Christmas Day with Mum.

He was going to Wetherby. We got him there just in time before carrying on south.)

I remember Arkle running his last race at Kempton. Even though the commemorative bronze of him stands at Cheltenham, I think of him more at Kempton where he broke down in the King George over thirty years ago. Desert Orchid brought back Arkle's days – the days when a racehorse really grabbed the public's imagination – and that old slugger was more at home at Kempton than Cheltenham, and not just in my mind. The statue of him that you see as you walk in through the main entrance is testimony to this. He was a great. He did it on guts.

Dessie had his first race at Kempton over hurdles as a headstrong novice. He fell and was down, winded, for more than twenty minutes. I think they even put the screens around him. I'm glad he caught his breath, for racing's sake, and also for my own two sons. Dessie was always stabled in the summer at his owners' – the Burridges – family farm in North Yorkshire, near where I went to school. We sneaked up to visit one year – before it became common knowledge that the farm was Dessie's summer hide-out – and my boys were allowed to sit on one of racing's most famous backs. I have a photo of the old boy with us that day.

Simon Sherwood is the jockey everyone remembers best on Dessie. Simon, who is now a successful trainer in partnership with his brother Oliver in Lambourn, won nine out of his ten rides on Desert Orchid, including the Gold Cup at Cheltenham. He was one of the four (five if you count Brian Rouse in a two-mile handicap on the flat) jockeys who partnered Dessie – Colin Brown, Graham Bradley and Richard Dunwoody complete the jumping quartet – and they were all brilliant in helping Channel 4 bring the joy of the horse at the racecourse to the programmes and the viewers at home. David Elsworth, Dessie's trainer, was, I'm the first to admit, also great. We visited his yard at Whitsbury many times to film the stable star. David's back there now, after a spell at Whitcombe where a number of trainers have been based recently. Dessie is in Yorkshire now, happily retired, but he has returned to Kempton to lead the parade and gallop past the Christmas crowds. Like Red Rum before him, who had the same relationship with Aintree, he opens betting shops and makes other public appearances.

Before Dessie, the Dickinsons had a great run in the King George. Tony, now sadly dead, Michael (who obviously recovered well enough from that twenty-first birthday party to have his brilliant career in jumping before Manton and America!), and Mrs Monica Dickinson – Mrs D to everyone – have all played a part in the race's history. During Dessie's era it was really only François Doumen who offered any challenge – and, in the process, proved Big Mac wrong about French jockeys. The competition he brought from France was great for the King George and for racing overall. Even the Festival. French horses used to come to Britain to win jumps races after the Second World War. By the eighties, though, the edge had gone until François Doumen emerged on the scene. His first success in the King George – Nupsala, in 1987 – stunned the Kempton crowd, many of whom had come to see Dessie win again. Instead it was André Pommier, not Colin Brown, Dessie's jockey, who picked off the prize after the front runners had gone off at a cracking pace. Four years later François saddled The Fellow to win the race again for France and he was ridden to victory by Adam Kondrat, whom Big Mac was constantly slagging off. The partnership also won the Gold Cup at

Cheltenham in 1994, after two near misses. The ride Kondrat gave The Fellow to win did more than just win a trophy: it actually shut Big Mac up, which is almost as big an achievement!

The workload of December means I miss out on some of the fun of the Christmas month. There's the Channel 4 party, when we all have a chance to let our hair down, streamers, party hats, the works, and I go to quite a few charity dinners around this time – Bob Champion's Cancer Trust, Riding for the Disabled (one of Julie's favourite charities for which Judith Walker does such great work), the Spinal Injuries' Association and Lord's Taverners' functions. But my commitments on the night – sometimes I'm asked to host an auction of racing memorabilia to raise funds or to make an after-dinner speech – and the general December daily racing schedule mean that I'm never the last to leave and often the first to head for the door – in the nicest possible way.

'Race nights' are popular in December. These are occasions where films of past races, with fictional, pre-recorded studio commentaries dubbed on, are screened and guests bet on the outcome blind with a share of the gambling going to a good cause. It amazes me that people bet without knowing what's running or having any form to go on but the charities benefit, which is the main thing. At first, when I was just starting out, I thought I did quite well out of the films, professionally speaking. As a young reporter, I was approached by a Marty Seligzon to provide voice-overs for some that his company, Beneficial Arts, was hoping to market in Britain. I was offered £5 a film and did twenty which, in those days, was big money for me. Overall, though, Marty did rather better than that. The films lasted about ten years, and he rented them out all over the world. He must have made millions, some of which went towards the purchase of the ocean-view house he has in California.

Christmas is, of course, a special occasion. I'm a great believer in the day itself, and all that it means to families everywhere. It's not an especially indulgent or alcoholic affair for us. Once I had two Christmas lunches, the first on a United Arab Emirates plane flying back from Dubai before going round to Bob Champion's for a second helping, but generally we spend it quietly. The one treat I'm always allowed (by Julie!) is to open the presents. But, like a lot of people in racing, especially those involved in the National Hunt game, I have to keep an eye on the next day's work. There's the Boxing Day *Morning Line* script, and a great afternoon's racing ahead, weather permitting. It's one of the biggest days of December – of the year. Got to be on the ball all year round.

New Year's Eve is the same. Remember, most years I'm the one who has to get up early the next day with a clear head for the afternoon's programme. There used to be a ball at Newmarket, similar to Julie's charity event in April, if not half as grand, which gave the town the chance to celebrate the passing of another twelve months and contemplate the next twelve ahead, but I was never able to enjoy it to the full. The racing calendar doesn't make any allowances for 31 December and all its traditions. It is, at best, a night on the orange juice for me. Sometimes I'm in bed by nine-thirty – in the evening, that is. Mind you, there are a few who, in the past, may have wished they'd done the same. Newmarket is a small town, with plenty of gossip. Even before I'm on my way to Cheltenham, the rumours of no-good goings on have started. As has another racing year – for you and me to enjoy. Another twelve months of excitement ahead, all over Britain, in Ireland, France, Dubai and maybe America, Australia and even Japan. Who knows what the New Year will bring? Never the same, always different. I wouldn't miss any of it. Not for the earth.

Index